EVEREST

FROM THE FIRST ATTEMPT
TO THE FINAL VICTORY

EVEREST

FROM THE FIRST ATTEMPT
TO THE FINAL VICTORY

By
Micheline Morin

With many illustrations in colour
and black-and-white and maps

PILGRIMS PUBLISHING
Varanasi◆Kathmandu

EVEREST: From the First Attempt to the Final Victory
Micheline Morin

Published by:
PILGRIMS PUBLISHING

An imprint of:
PILGRIMS BOOK HOUSE
B 27/98 A-8, Nawabganj Road
Durga Kund, Varanasi-221010, India
Tel: 91-542-314060, 312456
E-mail: pilgrims@satyam.net.in
Website: www.pilgrimsbooks.com

Distributed in India by:
PILGRIMS BOOK HOUSE
B 27/98 A-8, Nawabganj Road
Durga Kund, Varanasi-221010, India
Tel: 91-542-314060, 312456
E-mail: pilgrims@satyam.net.in
Website: www.pilgrimsbooks.com

Distributed in Nepal by:
PILGRIMS BOOK HOUSE
P O Box 3872, Thamel,
Kathmandu, Nepal
Tel: 977-1-424942
Fax: 977-1-424943
E-mail: pilgrims@wlink.com.np

Cover Design by Sasya

ISBN: 81-7769-180-5

Rs. 250/-

Printed in India

CONTENTS

ACKNOWLEDGMENT

The illustrations in this book have been redrawn from copyright photographs by permission of the Royal Geographical Society and the Alpine Club of Great Britain.

ILLUSTRATIONS

IN COLOUR

IN BLACK-AND-WHITE

    A*

MAPS

A SALUTE TO THE VICTORS

THIS is the astounding story of the efforts which men made for thirty-two years to conquer the highest mountain in the world.

It is the story, so to speak, of a gigantic human ladder. In the imagination a vision arises of white men and native Himalayans banded together and climbing upward year after year upon one another's shoulders, climbing each time a little higher, and gaining in boldness as they climb. Sometimes the structure totters, but the effort, though apparently wasted, goes to benefit those who follow after. And each man bends his head so that he who comes behind may stand upon his shoulders and climb yet higher, until the day when the enormous pyramid, finally completed, bears the latest-comers to the summit of the mountain.

All mountaineers have some experience of the human ladder, and they know that the man at the bottom merits as much praise as the man at the top. They form part, as it were, of a single body ; they share the same tension of mind and muscle as they struggle to keep their balance. And it is only just that in the hour of success they should take an equal pride in the achievement, for without each other they could have done nothing.

Thus, without in any way belittling the exploit of Hillary and Tenzing, it is fair to say that the 1953 victory is the victory of all the expedition leaders, climbers, members of support teams, transport officers, doctors, ' tigers ' (the cream of the native climbers), and last, but not least, the porters who took part in the ten successive expeditions. It is fitting, therefore, that we do honour to them all.

A.J.V.

CHAPTER I

GETTING TO KNOW A MOUNTAIN

THE story of Everest is undoubtedly far older than the history of man. Yet although in distant times its glaciers came lower down into the valleys than they do at present, the mountain was probably very similar in its general structure to the Everest we know to-day. Already it towered high above all other peaks, its sharp-edged ridges radiated outward in all directions, and its rocky walls fell sharply away into chasms of enormous depth.

For tens of thousands of years Everest reigned supreme in happy isolation, smiling upward in the clear morning sunshine or raising its terrible voice in time of storm, disturbed only by the lammergeier (or bearded vulture) and the jackdaw as they wheeled in the wind about its head, and in all likelihood by the mysterious ' Abominable Snowman ' who left his footprints on the glaciers of the lower slopes.

The question arises as to whether the short, yellow-skinned natives of the Everest region were acquainted with the mountain before it was first seen by white men. It does not stand out clearly to the naked eye. When seen from the summits of the Indian ranges, it merges into Kanchenjunga, forming with this and other mountains a great white mass which is only occasionally visible ; more often than not it is completely hidden by clouds.

On the Tibetan side Everest is even harder to find. Like the Barre des Ecrins, in the French Alps, it is masked by a number of outlying peaks and can be seen only on closer approach through the valleys.

We know that mountain-dwelling races have always, in their early history, dreaded the mountains among which they lived, and have carefully refrained from attempting to climb them. The Tibetans and the Nepalese are no exceptions to the rule. In the Alps hunters and crystal-gatherers were the first to brave the terrors of what were then known as the ' horrid peaks,' and it was in search of chamois and rock-crystal that they first came to climb the rocky slopes and make their way across the glaciers. The Tibetans and the Nepalese, however, are not hunting races. Their religion forbids them to kill animals, with the exception of certain domestic breeds. Nor do they gather crystals, the latter being apparently rare in their part of the world.

Sheer necessity led these peoples, in their efforts to establish communications between one side of the chain and the other, to open up tracks here and there across the Himalayas, crossing cols that rise to heights of up to 16,500 feet. The hardships which they encountered, however, from cold, wind, and storm, and the battles which such journeys entailed—sometimes they had to cut footholds for their yaks in the ice—could only deepen their horror of the great peaks.

This horror is revealed very strikingly in the Tibetan conception of Hell. Paintings found in monasteries show that for them Hell is no fiery furnace but an icy Gehenna into which the damned are pitched by a devil armed with a fork. It is nevertheless certain that curiosity overcame the fears of the little mountain folk, who pushed on far enough to catch a glimpse of the mountain. Otherwise why should they have named it Chomo-Lungma, the Goddess-Mother of the World ? The authenticity of the name, which the Tibetans, it is true, give rather to the Everest-Makalu massif as a

A.J.Y.

whole, is disputed in certain quarters, but maps drawn up by
Jesuits as early as 1717 and based upon locally obtained information
mention the name of Tchoumou-Lancma, while the Tibetan passport granted by the Dalai Lama to the first British expedition in
1921 certainly refers to the ' Chomo-Lungma Mountain ' as the
object of the visit to be made by a group of Europeans. In 1852
the Ordnance Survey of India had already been working for some
considerable time on a map of the Himalayas. Chomo-Lungma
figured thereon as a nameless point bearing the inscription ' Peak
XV.' Observations were taken with a view to determining its
height, and the necessary calculations were in progress when one
day an excited clerk burst into the office of the Director-General,
Sir Andrew Waugh, shouting, " Sir ! sir ! I've just discovered the
highest mountain in the world ! " According to his figures, it rose
to a height of 29,002 feet.

Fresh calculations were made later. It is difficult to obtain
accurate measurements in the neighbourhood of such high mountains : the Himalayan mass exerts a gravitational pull on surrounding bodies, rather like the action of the moon on the sea. Thus the
levelling device on a theodolite no longer indicates the horizontal,
nor does a plumb-line hang vertically. Instruments cease to
register accurately. Taking such deviations into account (and they
are far from negligible, amounting at one observation point near
Darjeeling to an angle of 51 seconds, or nearly a minute), calculations were resumed, and it was found that the highest mountain in
the world rose to a height of 29,028 feet. Certain British authorities,
however, for some unknown reason, continued to credit Everest
with a height of 29,002 feet as they had done previously, and
mountaineers in general have followed their lead in continuing to
recognize this height.

For some time Sir Andrew Waugh tried to discover whether
the mountain was known to the natives by some local name.
Having failed to do so, he finally gave it the name of his predecessor
as Director-General of the Ordnance Survey of India, Sir George
Everest. The name Everest has the advantage of being short and
easily pronounced in almost any language, and it has remained in
general use ever since.

Despite all this, European school-children continued to be
taught for years that the highest point in the Himalayas was Mt.
Gaurisankar. For this misunderstanding the blame must be laid
on two German explorers, the Schlagintweit brothers, who towards
1855 made the mistake of confusing the latter mountain with
Everest. The information which they brought back was recorded
in German atlases, and from there was passed on into the atlases

of neighbouring countries. The error persisted until corrected in 1903 by Captain Wood, who, after a visit to Nepal, proved

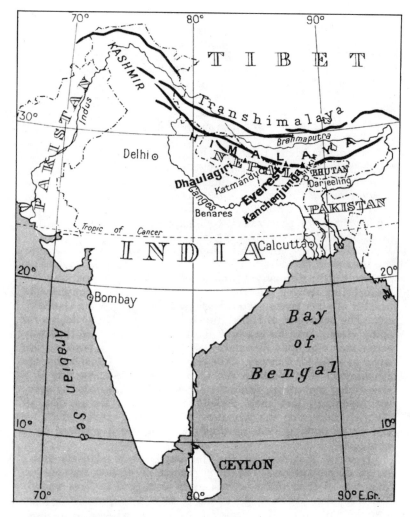

trigonometrically that the two entirely different peaks were more than thirty miles apart.

If we look at India on the map we shall find that it looks like a big bunch of grapes with the island of Ceylon apparently falling away from the stalk. To the north the bunch is solidly attached to the Asiatic continent, as it were, by the strong, gnarled branch of the Himalayas.

This chain of mountains has obviously lost its way in life. Instead of rising in Asia it should really have emerged in America, so famous for records of every kind. It is the longest chain in the world—1500 miles, or two and a half times the length of the Alps —and it includes the twenty-three highest mountains on earth.

Its name is derived from the Sanskrit word *hima*, meaning at once ' cold,' ' snow,' and ' winter,' and best translated by something like ' The Snowy One.' This expression is oddly akin to the name given to the range by the British in India, who called it ' The Snows.'

One must admit that both names are appropriate to the Himalayan chain as seen from Kipling's beloved ' Hills,' looming up as it does like a huge accumulation of snow and ice. Only the southern side is visible, and—just the opposite of what we find in the Alps—the southern face is more deeply covered in snow than the northern, as the former is directly exposed to precipitation from the monsoon.

Despite their tremendous height, the Himalayas do not form the watershed between India and Tibet. Two great rivers rising on their northern slopes, the Indus and the Brahmaputra, cross the chain before flowing into the Indian Ocean, as do a considerable number of other rivers—the Arun, the Tista, the Krishna Gandaki, etc. The behaviour of Himalayan rivers has puzzled geologists for many years ; how, for example, did they manage to find their way across such a gigantic mountain barrier ? Geologists, however, are never at a loss for a theory. The rivers, they say, existed before the Himalayas. The southern rim of the Tibetan plateau rose in a slow tilting movement, while the rivers quietly proceeded to carve the mountains into their present shape. This theory, like all theories concerning the formation of the earth—about which we can prove nothing—will no doubt last until it is replaced by a new one.

However that may be, the Himalayas are a relatively young range of mountains. The slow process of erosion has not yet rounded off their peaks or rubbed their rugged surfaces smooth. In its general contours the chain is at once impressive and be-wildering in its rapid alternations from one extreme to another, from knife-edged ridges and lofty peaks that stab upward at the sky to rocky walls that fall away to a depth of 10,000 feet and narrow, fissure-like valleys along which raging torrents go roaring on their way.

It is clear from accounts of the earliest expeditions that British geologists were treated with marked disfavour by the natives of Tibet, who objected strongly to the scientists' habit of hammering at rocks and breaking off specimen pieces. They claimed that as a result of this practice certain devils were set free and allowed to pass from an earlier world into the present one, and that this meant trouble for all concerned. They also found it hard to believe that the Europeans had no financial axe to grind. Perhaps those pieces of rock were really precious stones, were rubies, garnets, or were possibly even gold ? Suspicious eyes watched every movement, until finally one day a geologist found that a case of specimens had been stolen from him and replaced by a case of yak-dung : words simply failed the unfortunate scientist.

When the Ordnance Survey of India undertook the task of mapping the Himalayas they had no alternative but to call upon the services of mountaineers. Only they could overcome the natural barriers that stood in the way of the would-be explorer. The first British expeditions were thus geographical explorations rather than purely mountaineering exploits.

Climbers, however, can never say no to their favourite form of temptation, and the chance seemed too good to miss ; taking advantage of the scientific missions entrusted to them, the so-called explorers began climbing the Himalayan peaks. In 1818 the Lloyds reached a height of 19,030 feet. In 1855 the Schlagintweits made an attempt on Mt. Kamet (25,447 feet). From 1860 to 1870 Johnson made a series of climbs of over 19,500 feet.

These exploratory missions were then followed by genuine mountaineering expeditions. In 1883 Mt. Kabru, in the Kanchenjunga massif, was attempted by Graham, the Karakorams by Conway in 1892, in 1895 the famous Mummery attacked Nanga Parbat, where he was unfortunately killed, and in 1899 Freshfield tackled Kanchenjunga.

New hunting-grounds had now to be found, for by the end of the last century mountaineering—that wonderful game invented by the British—had come of age. The Alpine Club had been founded in 1857, Whymper had conquered the Matterhorn, and one by one all the great Alpine peaks had subsequently fallen.

Ambition thrives, of course, on success, and it now occurred to mountaineers that there was one mountain, the highest in the world, that no one had ever climbed.

There is not the slightest doubt that mountains present a permanent challenge to man. 'I dare you,' they seem to say to him as they proudly tower up into the blue sky, and we all know what to expect when man is confronted with invitations like that.

There has been, there still is, and there always will be a great deal of argument as to what it is that drives men to climb mountains. The best reason of all was given by Mallory—a simple reason, but one that includes all the others. Asked by a friend, why he was so keen to climb Mt. Everest, Mallory answered, " Because it's there."

A.J.V.

A.J.V.

PART I: THE APPROACH FROM THE NORTH

CHAPTER II

THE BEGINNINGS

THE first man to think seriously of sending an expedition to Everest was Captain (later Brigadier-General) the Hon. C. G. Bruce, who was talking of it as early as 1893, but when in 1903 he tried to organize a preliminary reconnaissance he immediately encountered a snag. The mountain stands on the frontier between Tibet and Nepal, and it was therefore absolutely essential to obtain permission from one country or the other to enter its territory. Permission was refused on both sides.

By 1913 the position seemed to have improved, and hopes ran

B

A Typical Himalayan Ridge

high once more, but with the breaking out of war in 1914 the whole project went back into the melting-pot.

Only in 1919 was the idea resurrected, when it was put forward at a meeting of the Royal Geographical Society and greeted with enthusiasm by the President of the Alpine Club and by British mountaineers in general. Negotiations were immediately opened by the two powerful organizations with a view to obtaining the permission hitherto refused. This time the Fates were to be kinder. It happened that the British political agent in Sikkim, Sir Charles Bell, was a personal friend of the Dalai Lama, and thus had freedom of access to Lhasa. Sir Charles was asked to present the necessary application. The Tibetan ruler, who is at the same time the spiritual head of his country, twice refused before allowing himself to be persuaded. At a third interview, however, he finally gave way and handed Sir Charles a passport recommending the British expedition to the officials in charge of the districts concerned. This rough, parchment-like piece of paper stated that a group of white men would be travelling " to the west of the Five Treasures of the Great Snow [i.e., the Kanchenjunga massif—Translator] in the jurisdiction of the Fort of the Shining Glass near the Monastery of the Valley of Deep Ravines in the Southern Land of Birds "— a delightful if rather long-winded way of saying that certain Europeans would be travelling through Southern Tibet. Every Oriental, of course, is something of a poet for whom time is of no account.

News of the successful issue of the negotiations reached London early in January 1921, and the Everest organizations immediately went into action.

They had plenty of work on their hands. First of all money had to be found, so a fund was launched by the Royal Geographical Society and by the Alpine Club. Then agreements were made with various newspapers and magazines regarding payment for publication rights, covering telegrams and photographs from the expedition. Finally the Duke of Windsor (then Prince of Wales) was good enough to support the undertaking by forwarding a generous contribution. From now on the expedition was on a sound financial footing.

At the same time a ' Mount Everest Committee ' was formed, and its first task was to appoint a leader for the expedition. Bruce, now a general, was not available, and his place was taken by Lieutenant-Colonel C. K. Howard-Bury, who, although not a climber himself, had done a great deal of hunting in the Himalayas. He was familiar with Asiatics, and got on well with them ; this seemed an excellent qualification for the leadership.

B*

Long arguments ensued as to what the object of the expedition was to be. For the Royal Geographical Society the main aim was to collect topographical, geological, and botanical data. For the Alpine Club the object was to climb Everest. A compromise was reached, and it was decided that a thorough reconnaissance of the massif would be carried out in order to find the easiest route to the top, while the scientists would carry on with their research. Needless to say, the mountaineers secretly hoped to do more than a mere reconnaissance and intended to climb Everest if an opportunity presented itself.

The next step was to get together a mountaineering team, including an assault group of four climbers. A list of ' possibles ' was carefully studied, and two experienced men with a number of Himalayan climbs to their credit—Raeburn and Dr Kellas—were picked. Then two young climbers were added, men who had already shown what they were made of in the Alps : these were Mallory and his former schoolfellow, Bullock.

Mallory, the son of a clergyman, was in private life a master at a public school. Physically he was a tall, handsome, regular-featured young man ; he possessed extraordinary stamina, and in the mountains moved at such a pace that his companions had difficulty in keeping up with him. Mentally, he was refined, cultured, and sensitive to the beauties of Nature. He was to reveal himself a determined and strong-willed man of irresistible drive and enthusiasm tempered by sound judgment.

To the surprise of all concerned he showed no particular sign of pleasure when the President of the Alpine Club, Captain Farrar, informed him that he had been chosen. His real feelings became apparent on the day when, asked whether in the actual assault on the summit he would mind sharing a sleeping-bag at 26,000 feet, he exclaimed, " I'll sleep with *anybody* as long as I get to the top ! "

The team was then brought up to full strength by the addition of Wollaston, a naturalist and doctor, Morshead and Wheeler, two surveyors from the Indian Ordnance Service, and Dr Heron, a geologist, making nine in all.

CHAPTER III

FORMING UP FOR THE ATTACK

TRAVEL by air had not yet become an everyday event, and the members of the expedition made their way to India by rail and by sea. Early in May they were all assembled at Darjeeling. About a hundred miles from Everest, Darjeeling is a hill station (approximately 7000 feet) to which Europeans come regularly to recover from the exhausting tropical heat of the Indian plains. This ' rest area ' lies on the summit of a fold in the pre-Himalayan uplands known as ' The Hills.' The surrounding greenery makes a setting of unusual beauty, and when the sky is clear to the north —a rare event—an excellent view can be had of the fabulous Himalayas. Draped in white, with their rocky foundations cloaked, in mist, they seem to float in the sky, detached from the earth. The nearest—and in some ways the most remarkable—peak is

Kanchenjunga (28,146 feet), only forty miles away as the crow flies. Everest itself is so far away to the north that identification becomes difficult.

Before leaving Darjeeling the expedition had to arrange transport for rations and equipment. Pack-animals (a hundred mules) were lent by the Indian Government, and a certain number of porters had to be provided in addition.

This business of working out the number of porters required is nothing like as easy as it might seem at first sight. It is certainly not enough merely to divide the weight of the gear as a whole by the weight of the average individual load. Once you have worked that out, you then realize that you've forgotten to take the porters' food into account. This extra load means that you have to allow for extra porters, who will then need feeding in their turn, etc. .

A.J.V.

I shall never forget watching the Committee of the French Expedition of 1936 struggling with these mathematical Chinese puzzles, to the huge delight of a certain privileged few ! Colonel Howard-Bury simplified the problem by hiring there and then about fifty Sherpas and arranging to engage the others in Tibet, as and when they were needed. The Sherpas are descended from a Tibetan tribe which settled long ago in Nepal—small, slit-eyed men, accustomed to carry heavy loads from childhood onward, and whose muscular bodies never seem to tire. Warm clothing, including Balaclava helmets, gloves, etc., was issued to them, but when it came to footgear trouble began with a vengeance, as some of them had feet as broad as they were long!

Finally, a number of ponies were reserved for the use of the white men, who, if they had to toughen up on the way to the mountain, also had to keep something in reserve for the final ordeal.

The most direct route from Darjeeling to Everest crosses Nepal in a westerly direction. Admission to Nepal having been refused, the expedition first moved off to the east and then carried out a huge encircling movement through Southern Tibet so as to reach the mountain from the north. This march of nearly three hundred miles, with the porters, and frequently the British, too, travelling on foot, took four or five weeks to accomplish.

One of the biggest obstacles to be overcome by any expedition is bad weather. The Himalayas form a climatic barrier between the high plateaux of India and those of Central Asia, and they receive as a result the full fury of the prevailing winds. Every summer the bad weather works up to the crisis known as the monsoon.

The latter is due to the storms and barometric depressions set up in the hot sea-areas of the Bay of Bengal. Laden with moisture, the monsoon moves northward, crosses the burning plains of India, and suddenly meets the ice-cold Himalayas, where it condenses in heavy rain. It is a seasonal phenomenon whose behaviour can be plotted in advance. When the monsoon's arrival is reported from Ceylon it is safe to assume that it will reach the North of India three weeks later. Blowing from the south-east, it generally reaches Everest between the 6th and the 10th of June. For about three months it drenches the mountain in clouds and covers it with tons of melting snow. And then people grumble about bad weather in the Alps ! Thus during the summer months, which are generally the most favourable for mountain climbing, on account of the warm weather and long hours of daylight, any attempt on Everest is right out of the question. The only period of fine weather during which there is any reasonable prospect of climbing the mountain comes between the end of the cold season and the onset of the monsoon, a spell of about three weeks, and even this is sometimes broken by passing storms. Time is therefore strictly limited for the conquest of the highest mountain in the world. One can see at once why all Everest expeditions have been carried out with such a sense of urgency, and the surprising thing is that sheer haste should not have caused more disasters than has been the case.

The peculiarities of the monsoon have but gradually become clear from observations made and reported by successive expeditions ; they were only known in part by the team preparing to set out on May 18. This expedition was to help to provide precise details of local conditions.

A.J.V

CHAPTER IV

THE 1921 EXPEDITION

The Approach

THE assembled column of pack-animals and men—some of the latter on foot, some on horseback—finally set out from Darjeeling and made its way through the tea-plantations before dipping down into the valley of the Tista. The latter is extremely deep, and the river itself a mere 650 feet above sea-level.

As the ' caravan ' gradually lost height it dropped deeper and deeper into dense forest, where it once more ran into the moist heat of the Indian plains. The men were soon streaming with sweat, but dared not remove their sticky clothing for fear of mosquitoes. Fortunately, their attention was distracted by the remarkable spectacle of the tropical vegetation through which they were passing, and this helped them to forget their discomfort.

The magnificent forests of Sikkim are rightly famous. Arbores-
cent ferns grow literally to the stature of trees, and the trees themselves rise to a height of 150 feet. Some of them are smooth-
trunked, others are covered in thick, fleece-like masses of white
orchids. Pepper-plants and tropical creepers twine together and
sprawl from branch to branch, curl themselves into tangled skeins
and then reach out again, coil here and there round festoons of
blossom or hang down to the ground like long ropes. So dense is
the foliage that it forms a sort of natural crypt, within which
everything is shrouded in a semi-darkness made still more eerie by
a mist which makes solid objects appear to recede and blurs every
outline, while the general humidity turns the entire forest into a
soggy, dripping mass of reeking vegetation.

A vivid sense of palpitating life is conveyed by the rapid growth
of all this vegetation—so rapid that it hardly seems normal—and
by the carnivorous flowers, the teeming insects, the swarms of
multicoloured butterflies that feed just as readily on the carcases
of dead animals as on the flowers with their blossoms of brilliant red.

Down and down the expedition went until it reached the river-
bed. The Tista, which with its tributaries drains the whole of
Sikkim, has the volume of a major river and the fury of a mountain
torrent. It dashes itself with a roar like thunder against the walls
that hem it in, hurls itself at the masses of rock that stand in its
way, breaks over them, and races on in a seething, spouting mass
of water that fills the twisting gorge with steaming mist.

Fortunately, the obstacle is crossed by a crude suspension bridge,
and the expedition passed over without incident before beginning
to climb for the first time to higher ground.

They were now on the centuries-old caravan-route, the route
to Lhasa ; this they were to follow for some time, rising progressively
as the track climbed up and up to the high plateaux of Tibet.
There they were to meet caravans bringing down bales of wool
and others taking up corn, rice, copper, and manufactured goods.
The swarthy muleteers wore turquoise earrings, and greeted the
party with friendly smiles.

As they gradually gained height they moved through the many
varieties of a constantly changing flora ; it was as though they
were travelling from the Tropics to the Pole. At Kalimpong they
found scarlet hibiscus, clumps of daturas, their enormous flowers
gleaming in the dark and giving off a penetrating scent, bougain-
villeas, and a profusion of mauve, white, and yellow orchids.

Climbing higher and higher, they entered the gorgeous realm
of the rhododendron—not the humble shrub of the Alps, but a
tree bedecked with magnificent flowers. Every possible colour was

seen : pink, crimson, yellow, purple, white, and cream. The hollows of the valleys were carpeted with their multicoloured blossoms. Among them grew modest flowers that heralded a cooler climate to come : pink saxifrages, and primulas of a reddish-purple hue. It was just as though India, like some fairy in a story-book, were lavishing all her charms and treasures on these men from the outside world, to attract them to her and make them her prisoners for ever.

Unfortunately, there was another side to that delightful picture. Rainfall is heavy in Sikkim, and the rain brings out myriads of

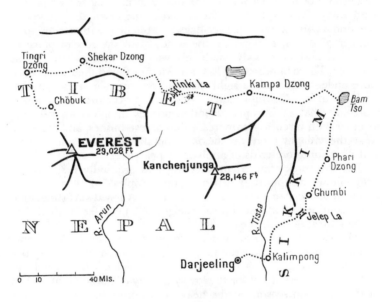

The Approach March through Sikkim and Tibet

leeches, which lie in wait on bushes and stones by the wayside, ready to attach themselves to anyone who might brush against them as they pass. Great care was necessary, as the resultant sores tended to fester easily.

Still climbing, the expedition reached Jelep La, or the Jelep Col, 14,390 feet high, on the very frontier of Tibet, and immediately they ran into the teeth of the wind. Every expedition that has travelled through Tibet has complained of the wind. Each day it blows unceasingly, from ten o'clock in the morning till midnight. It varies in violence, but is always bitterly cold. Moreover, it dries the ground as it goes along, raising the dust in swirling clouds.

As the dust is picked up from ground full of microbes—sanitation being unknown in Tibet—it has been held responsible for the throat troubles that the members of every expedition have suffered from in the past. It is believed by some that the germ-laden dust sets up an infection which is later aggravated by unusually rapid breathing in an ice-cold atmosphere. Bacteria themselves, however, are susceptible to cold, and it would perhaps be wise to regard the theory as ' not proven.'

Tibet now lay at the feet of the British climbers, but they could see nothing of it on account of the mist and melting snow that the wind was driving into their faces. Near the cairn that serves as a boundary-mark the ' prayer-flags,' [1] attached with string to a number of staves, fluttered in the wind. Not the sort of place to linger in, and everybody made his way downhill as smartly as possible. Three hundred feet lower down they found themselves once more under a blue sky, a sight they had not seen for weeks on end.

Here in the Chumbi valley (see map, p. 31) the vegetation is more like that of Europe. Rhododendrons mingle with fir-trees, together with birches, sycamores, willows, rose-bushes, and clematis. Near the villages there are fields of potatoes, wheat, and barley, and flourishing orchards of apple- and pear-trees.

But the track climbed up and up, and gradually firs, birches, and willows disappeared. Irises, blue poppies, white anemones, and primulas became more and more rare. A few dwarf rhododendrons contined to appear up to a height of 13,000 feet ; then they in their turn gave up the struggle.

The caravan was now moving forward over the high Tibetan plateau, whose enormous undulations rise and fall between 13,000 and 16,500 feet. It is a bare and desolate region which would be truly sinister were it not for the lovely quality of the sunlight. Only in the monsoon season do the heavy rains cross the Himalayas to pour down on the Indian plains, and in early spring the dry atmosphere is wonderfully transparent. Foreground and background stand out sharp and clear in all their wealth of colour. The ochre-tinted hills are silhouetted against an azure sky, and the snow-covered summits are clearly reflected in lakes that alternate from blue to green. In summer the scene changes. A light haze restores depth to the landscape, and the great mountains with their stretches of blue shadow fade away into the mysterious distance.

There are relatively few animals in Tibet, owing to the sparseness of the vegetation, but besides herds of domesticated yaks there are wild animals too—wild asses, sheep, gazelles, marmots, and hares. In addition there are considerable numbers of birds, such as sky-

[1] *Translator's Note :* See opposite.

larks, finches, partridges, and rock - martins, not to mention the bearded lammergeier, half-eagle, half - vulture, which has unfortunately disappeared from the French Alps, in spite of the resolution passed every year at the General Meeting of the Club Alpin Français in favour of its preservation. In Tibet wild animals have no fear of

human beings, as the Tibetan people never hunt them, and they live cheek by jowl with man on terms of almost easy familiarity.

Like all regions high above sea-level, Tibet is a land of extreme temperatures, being hot by day and bitterly cold by night, so every morning the expedition made an effort to start off early in order to get under canvas before nightfall ; camp was usually set up near the villages.

Tibetan houses are built of *pisé*, or puddled clay, a material that stands up well to very dry climates such as that of Tibet, which is protected by the Himalayas from the rain-laden monsoon. At the entrance to each village high masts rise into the air, and to these are nailed bands of cloth on which innumerable prayers are printed. The wind as it blows them to and fro ' recites ' the prayers, and wafts their beneficent influence far and wide. *Om Mani Padme Hum !* (Hail, O jewel, lotus-borne !) *Om Mani Padme Hum !* What a lovely idea to ' broadcast ' prayer in this way ! And yet the Tibetan method seems somehow to verge on cheating, like the prayer-wheels which the lamas and other pious people absent-mindedly turn as a form of worship.

In 1921 power in Tibet was still shared by the civil servants and the lamas ; the latter are very numerous, and in consequence powerful. Polyandry still exists, and if, for example, the eldest of four brothers marries, his wife belongs by law to the other three as well.

People often quote as an example of the backwardness of Tibet the fact that the wheel proper is still unknown in that country. But how many realize that in France, in the Maritime Alps, there are places where a wheelbarrow is never seen ? What use would anyone have for a barrow in a district where streets are built like flights of steps and villages cling like birds' nests to the mountain-side ? And, by the same token, what could the Tibetans do with a wheeled vehicle on those mountain tracks of theirs ?

Thanks to that famous passport from the Dalai Lama, every-where the expedition halted they received a warm welcome from the local *Dzongpen*, a functionary whose title means literally ' Commander of the Fortress,' and who was of great assistance in helping to find fresh horses and pack-animals. Gradually the baggage-mules were replaced by yaks, the latter being better adapted to the rigours of the local climate.

The yak is a sort of domesticated buffalo with a superb spread of horns ; owing to the thick fleece that hangs down to his hooves, he always seems to be wearing an overcoat. He is luckily an easy-going creature, for otherwise his strength would make him a dangerous customer. Outstanding as a beast of burden, he carries heavy loads and can keep going for twelve hours on end without turning a hair. He can negotiate difficult ground, and if necessary swim across rivers. But he is slow. The yak is a philosopher ; he keeps up a steady two miles an hour, and nothing will ever persuade him to go any faster. He grazes on sparse grass—dry, frozen stuff that no other animal would look at—and you see him chewing his cud in driving snow that leaves icicles sticking to his coat. He looks as if he were carrying the cares of the world on his shoulders, but his doleful expression conceals a nature that is waggish and sly. In playful mood he will cast his burden down and start frisking about as if he had gone mad. You then have quite a job restoring him to a sense of duty—he's so strong ! The yak is certainly a godsend to the native of Tibet, who turns his milk into butter, yogurt, and cheese, weaves cloth from his hairy coat, uses his dung for fuel, his flesh for food, his horns as domestic utensils, and his hoofs for glue. So the Tibetan peasant is no less attached to his yak than is the Arab to his camel.

Tibet is a country of lavish hospitality, and the local *Dzongpen* would often invite the members of the British expedition to a meal. Into the dirty and smelly Tibetan houses they would go, to be introduced first to Tibetan tea ; this is more like broth than the

English variety, the taste of tea being largely cancelled out by the rancid butter with which it is mixed. Some of the party were unable to do it justice. There was also *tsampa*, a thickish broth of barley flour—the staple food of the natives—and local delicacies like sweet biscuits fried in butter. Drinks consisted of *chang*, a sort of beer brewed from barley, and *arrack*, an alcoholic liquor distilled from *chang* and resembling marc-brandy or home-made ' hooch.'

The general health of the expedition was far from satisfactory. Every one had been sorely tried by the damp heat of the tropical forests through which they passed ; they now had trouble with dysentery, caused partly by the change of diet and partly by the dirty habits of the native cooks. The latter refused to boil water and milk, and were often caught in the act of spitting on dirty dishes and wiping them with the tail of their shirt.

The hardest hit was Dr Kellas, who had hardly got back from exploring in Sikkim when, without any chance of an adequate rest, he had joined the expedition at Darjeeling. On arrival at Phari Dzong he had to go to bed, and before long he was unable even to mount his horse. From then on he had to be carried in a litter. Kellas was doomed never to recover ; soon afterwards, while crossing a col before Kampa Dzong, he died of heart-failure. It was not long before Raeburn too fell sick and had to be sent back to Sikkim. Thus, before the actual assault on Everest had even begun, the mountain had already taken its toll. Fate had struck particularly heavily at the assault group, which was now reduced to two—Mallory and Bullock.

Mallory was very impatient to see Everest, and his first chance came on the day of Kellas's burial at Kampa Dzong (see map, p. 31). On returning from the ceremony he went up on to the high ground above the village and there caught sight of the mountain. He described it as " a prodigious white fang, excrescent from the jaw of the world." The lower parts of the mountain being masked by intermediary ranges, however, he could see only the summit, and so arranged to make a forward reconnaissance with the object of obtaining a closer view.

A few days later, with Bullock and a handful of porters, he left the rest of the expedition and they made their way through a number of valleys and deep ravines before climbing upward along a rocky crest. When finally they came to a halt they found themselves looking down into the blue depths of the Arun valley. But above them, just where Everest should have been, there was nothing to be seen but clouds. Then, as they both stood gazing intently through their binoculars, the longed-for miracle occurred. Gradually the gleam of snow appeared through the mist, and the mountain came into view. "Gradually, very gradually," wrote Mallory, "we saw the great mountain-sides and glaciers and *arêtes*, now one fragment and now another through the floating rifts, until, far higher in the sky than imagination had ever dared to suggest, the white summit of Everest appeared. . . ."[1]

Everest had certainly made the most of its first public appearance. As if to make as great an impression as possible, the mountain had chosen to show itself in all the fantastic splendour of its cloudy raiment ; it was as though by showing itself gradually it meant to preserve something of its mystery and to excite the imagination to still wilder flights of fancy. Despite his emotion Mallory did not fail to make certain observations regarding the structure of the mountain. He noted that the northern ridge did not seem, at first sight, impossibly steep ; also that it was concave in outline, which suggested that it was connected by a col to a neighbouring ridge. Pleased with these scraps of information, Mallory and Bullock then rejoined the main party, which was pushing on to Shekar Dzong (see map, p. 31).

This is the most remarkable place on the entire route followed by the British expedition. Built on the flanks of a rocky peak about 980 feet in height, it reminds one of a larger version of the Mont Saint-Michel. The village itself lies at the foot, the monastery stands half-way up, and near the summit the fortress clings to the rock, connected by a wall to a tower sticking up on top like a lightning-conductor. The place as a whole is called in the Tibetan language ' The Hill of the Shining Glass,' a most appropriate name, for from a distance the light-coloured rock and the white buildings form one great luminous mass.

The arrival of the foreign ' caravan ' was greeted with eager curiosity at Shekar Dzong, the inhabitants never having seen Europeans before. As the place is of a fair size, it was decided to call a halt and to rest there for a while.

This stay allowed some of the expedition to visit the local· monastery, which is quite big, housing four hundred monks. It is formed of buildings built terrace-fashion one above the other, and connected by staircases and corridors hollowed out of the rock itself. The party visited the interior of the temple, braving in the process the almost overpowering smell of butter burning in tiny lamps.

Tibet is not only a land of howling winds, it is also a land of butter. The people eat copious amounts of butter, and they make offerings of butter to the gods, both by burning it in bowl-shaped lamps which are never allowed to go out, or by moulding the butter

[1] In Lieutenant-Colonel C. K. Howard-Bury, D.S.O., *Mount Everest : The Reconnaissance, 1921* (Arnold, 1922), p. 186.

into artistically carved and perforated designs.   These ornaments put one in mind of the waxen decorations on the candles carried in the South of France by young worshippers at their first Communion.

Like all Tibetan sanctuaries, the temple was dark inside and impressively quiet.   Gilded statues of Buddha, decorated with turquoises and other precious stones, softly gleamed in the dim light of butter-burning lamps.   Among them was another and much more imposing statue of Buddha, the face of which was gilded in similar style, and at the feet of the god [1] silver teapots and other pieces of richly decorated silverware were laid out as offerings.

On leaving the temple the visitors asked permission to see the Chief Lama, who is deeply revered, being looked upon as the reincarnation of an earlier priest.   The old man appeared in a robe of gold brocade enriched with splendid ornaments in Chinese silk. Although he had only one tooth in his head, his smile was delightful and the monks finally persuaded him to sit for his photograph on a dais, complete with his bell.   The monks had never seen a camera before, but they had heard of them, and were all agog with curiosity.

On the following day the advance was resumed in the direction of Tingri (see map, p. 27).   On the way there, the expedition met a Mongol pilgrim who had left Lhasa a year before and was making his way to Nepal measuring the length of the road as he went by using his own body as a yardstick.   His method of locomotion was like that of the ' looper-worm ' ;   he kept throwing himself face downward on the ground, then he would get up, place his feet wherever his hands came to rest, and once again stretch himself out on the ground.   Some pilgrims make things worse for themselves by lying down, not in the direction of the road itself, but at right angles to their line of travel.

Not all Tibetans, however, are so pious or so fanatical.   At Lhasa, where the inhabitants are expected once a year to measure with their own bodies the distance round the Holy City, they pay professional crawlers to act as substitutes.   According to Heinrich Harrer,[2] one of them had been making his way round the town like this every day for forty years.   That particular crawler, however, was an artful dodger ;   wearing a leather apron and padded gloves, he would take a running jump each time so as to get as far forward as possible !

At Tingri, where the expedition arrived a month after leaving Darjeeling, Mallory learnt that to the south there was a long valley, the valley of Rongbuk, that led straight to Everest, so, leaving the

[1] *Translator's Note :* Gautama Buddha is not, strictly speaking, regarded as a god, and Buddhists do not actually pray to him.
[2] *Seven Years in Tibet* (Rupert Hart-Davis, 1953).

The Forest of Sikkim

caravan to get on with its research work and scientific observations, he set off with Bullock and sixteen bearers.

The valley in question is certainly one of the bleakest spots in the world. Rocky, dusty, ice-cold, and bare of vegetation, it is none the less inhabited. At a height of 16,000 feet is found a little collection of houses and a monastery sheltering a score of lamas. At a still greater height there are hermits, both male and female, living alone in cells carved out of the mountain. Devoting themselves to spiritual exercises and contemplation, their sufferings must be terrible in winter, for they have neither fire nor anything hot to drink. If they do not succumb it is because Tibetans have quite exceptional powers of resistance to cold.

Poorly endowed by Nature, the Rongbuk Valley can, however, boast the finest ornament of all—Mt. Everest itself. It fills the whole of the background—an enormous white shape towering majestically like a god in all his glory, in the V-shaped framework of the valley. There Everest stands, reigning in solitary majesty over the rest of the world, one prodigious mass, every visible line of which gives an impression of power in perfect balance. The holy lamas and the hermits knew what they were doing, after all, when they came to the foot of Everest to meditate on the frailty and the insignificance of man.

The Reconnaissance of the Northern and Western Slopes

It has often been said that Everest expeditions have consisted of " reconnaissance, reconnaissance and still more reconnaissance." This definition applies to the 1921 expedition more aptly than to any other. Mallory and Bullock certainly found it necessary to study the different slopes of the mountain in order to determine the best, and possibly the one and only, route to the summit. It was an enormous task. Even the approach to Everest is an expedition in itself, demanding the setting up of several camps. A complete circuit of the mountain means travelling considerable distances, as the summit is connected to neighbouring peaks by huge ridges and high cols. From Rongbuk, Mallory at last had a full view of the northern face, and he could hardly drag himself away from such an awe-inspiring vision of overpowering mass and heavy, yet simple and clean-cut lines. The glacier leading towards the northern face rises gently, forming a sort of floor from which the mountain rises like a wall. From base to summit the face measures over 9200 feet. It was originally thought to be entirely covered in ice, for it had never been seen otherwise than white.

But the face presents in fact a rocky surface. Beneath its thin coating of snow the horizontal stratifications stand out clearly to the naked eye, causing the base to appear still broader, and emphasizing its appearance of solidity and power.

When mountaineers are seeking a new way up the side of a mountain they usually begin by picking a line from the summit downward. Suitable approaches are few and far between on the upper slopes, and it is on these that the rest of the route depends.

From his camping-ground at 16,400 feet Mallory studied the possibilities which the mountain seemed to offer. Two routes seemed capable of leading to the summit, apart from the face itself,

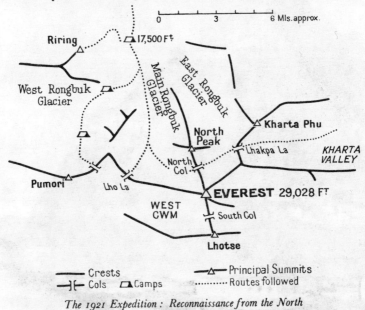

The 1921 Expedition : Reconnaissance from the North

which was out of the question. To the right there was the West Ridge, but this meant crossing an endless expanse of ground. To the left was the East Ridge, from which ran another and less jagged ridge dropping abruptly towards the north and apparently linking up with a sharp-pointed peak by means of a col (see map above).

The longer Mallory looked the more he realized that the climb would not be, as he had first thought, a steady march up long, snow-covered slopes : the going would be hard. He therefore decided to carry out a preliminary reconnaissance.

During the preceding day he had devoted some time to the training of inexperienced porters in rock-climbing, in the technique of walking through snow, and in the use of rope and ice-axe.

C

Shekar Dzong

While so doing he had noticed that in the Himalayas glaciers were not the quickest and most convenient means of gaining height, their surface being too rugged and broken. They are in fact a solid mass of swelling rises, ravines, pinnacles, and colossal towers of ice between which the climber must thread his way in an endless up-and-down progression. On those glaciers a man feels like some tiny Alpine flea faced with crevasses of the Mer de Glace !

Then again, the track is often blocked by the projections rising from the ice of the glacier and known by the South American term, *nieve penitentes*. Like the figments of some insane imagination, they seem to be moving along in droves, leaning forward on the march like crowds of refugees fleeing before an invading army. These are not true ' seracs,' since unlike the latter they are not so much poised on end as firmly rooted in the ice below them : they are more like enormous stalagmites of ice, rising sometimes to a height of fifty feet. There is some doubt as to their formation, but they are said to be due originally to boulders, which on becoming warmed by the sun are thought to produce in the ice beside them a sort of glacial excrescence which, once it has appeared, grows steadily bigger. As for the ' forward ' lean of the ' penitents,' this is apparently caused by the fact that the southern slope is exposed to the sun for longer periods than the rest of the mountain.

As Mallory and his companions made their way through this icy maze during the warmest part of the day they had their first experience of what later came to be known as a ' glacier tiredness.' They were overcome by a feeling of discomfort and extreme fatigue, a form of mountain-sickness which although well known has never as yet been explained. It is experienced by many people on Mont Blanc as they cross the shut-in zones of the Petit and Grand Plateaux. Can this be due to the harmful effect of the ice ? The feeling often disappears when one reaches the exposed open spaces of the Bosses ridge. On the Rongbuk Glacier, Mallory and his companions found that the symptoms wore off as soon as they left the hollows in the ice and began to move over the crest of the moraine.

The object of the first reconnaissance was to reach the head of the Rongbuk Glacier at the foot of the north face. Mallory wished to see : (1) whether it was possible to climb to the North Col via the western slope ; (2) whether it was possible to get a footing on the West Ridge ; (3) whether there was a col which would give access to the south side of Everest. Unfortunately, the weather was unfavourable, with clouds rising on every side. Mallory had just enough time to catch sight of the slopes leading to the North Col. These seemed too steep to allow continuous freedom of movement to large teams of porters ; if, therefore, it

c*

were decided that the route via the North Col was the most suitable, another line of approach to the Col would have to be found.

The second reconnaissance took place within the framework of the West Rongbuk Glacier. (See map, p. 41.) This time Mallory and Bullock were anxious to climb one of the neighbouring peaks in order to obtain a better view. From the top of Mt. Riring (22,500 feet), which they reached with some difficulty, as they were not sufficiently acclimatized, they obtained a sideways view of the North Ridge of Everest. This view confirmed their first impression ; the ridge was not very steep, and should be climbable. They also examined the peak which is separated from Everest by the North Col, and which, in view of its geographical position, they named Changtse—The North Peak. They tried to guess what lay behind it, and here they made an error of judgment which was to cost them dear. They thought that this ridge—of which only the top was visible, running eastward from the peak— lay parallel to a glacier, and that the latter would flow straight into the river Arun. Not for one moment did it occur to them that this ridge might stop short and the glacier turn northward, which in fact it does. Thus when later they set out to reach the glacier at its lowest point they thought it necessary to make an enormous detour.

They now decided to reconnoitre the actual floor of the West Rongbuk Glacier, hoping to find there some means of getting around the West Ridge so as to reach the south side of Everest from the rear. An advanced camp was established on the glacier, but bad weather prevented further progress for several days.

Nevertheless they ventured out in spite of snow and mist, and after a gruelling march reached a sort of spur on the edge of a deep precipice. They had no idea where they were, but assumed that they must have reached a col on the Nepalese frontier. They waited for a short time, hoping that the weather would clear and allow them to fix their position, but in view of the cold and the gathering clouds they made their way back to camp.

During the next few days they remained in the vicinity of the camp, teaching their porters to use snow-shoes, which were formerly used instead of skis in deep snow. This demands training, owing to the fatigue otherwise entailed by having to walk with the feet apart. Some enthusiasts, however, enjoyed walking on snow-shoes, and used to get up a fair speed by gliding downhill. Mallory himself considered that snow-shoes were a handicap when it came to jumping across crevasses.

As soon as the weather permitted he set off on a photographic reconnaissance, climbed a sort of rocky promontory standing out from a spur on the frontier chain, which he named ' The Island,'

and from there looked out over the surrounding country. He was beginning to suspect the existence of the West Cwm, " the mysterious Cwm lying in cold shadow," [1] carved in the southern flank of Everest. It is indeed strange that right from the beginning Mallory was

A.J.V.

attracted to that West Cwm, as if he had had a presentiment that there he would find the route that led to victory.

He was determined to make an attempt to reach the Cwm, and one day he set out in the early hours by the light of a full moon,

[1] Howard-Bury, *op. cit.*, p. 213. (Mallory used the Welsh spelling, having climbed a great deal in Wales.—*Translator.*)

and with the mountains casting their dark shadows over the glacier. " An exciting walk," as he put it, for he feared that the clouds still lingering here and there in the sky might close in and ruin everything. On the contrary : when at 5 A.M. the two men reached a col on the frontier range the view was superb. At last they were able to look down into the West Cwm, still ice-bound and grey in the shadow of Everest. To their great disappointment, however, they found it impossible to reach the Cwm, for a precipice over 1600 feet deep gaped at their very feet. For a time they stood gazing at the magnificent spectacle of an unknown group of mountains to the south. " It's a big world," was Mallory's comment.

This expedition brought the reconnaissance of the western and northern slopes of Mount Everest to a close. It had now been established that the major ridges were all impassable, with the exception of the northern one. The problem was therefore how to reach the foot of the ridge in question. This would involve climbing up the North Col, and as the western slope of the latter had been discovered to be very dangerous another route must be found up the other side on the eastern slope.

Mallory and Bullock immediately struck camp and returned to base. However, they were prevented from immediately beginning their new reconnaissance, Mallory having received a message from Howard-Bury telling him that all the photographs which he had taken were failures. He had put the plates into the camera the wrong way round ! He had thus to piece all his information together again as best he could.

While he was still reconnoitring the basin of the West Rongbuk Glacier Bullock seized the opportunity to carry out the first ascent of Lho La, a col at the foot of the West Ridge (see map, p. 41).

Finally the two mountaineers came down and rejoined Colonel Howard-Bury and the rest of the expedition. If only it had occurred to Mallory, as he was crossing the junction of the eastern glacier and the main Rongbuk Glacier, to push on with his reconnaissance to the head of the eastern branch of the glacier he would have saved himself a great deal of trouble, for he would immediately have found the quickest route to the North Col. But how could he have known that the little stream flowing out of the ice at that point drained a major glacier ? And in view of what he had seen from Mt. Riring, how could he have guessed that the glacier to the east of the North Col flowed into the main glacier ?

The Reconnaissance of the East Side

While Mallory and Bullock were exploring the Rongbuk Glacier, the rest of the expedition had covered the ground to the north of

Everest, preparing maps, botanizing, collecting specimens, and making scientific observations. Then, some time in July, Colonel Howard-Bury had moved his headquarters to the charming Kharta valley (see map, p. 41).

There he was met by Mallory and Bullock. No more suitable setting could have been chosen for these weary mountaineers, who were in urgent need of rest and a change of diet ; they were delighted to see fields, flowers, trees, and harvests once again.

After idling about for some time, Mallory and Bullock reminded themselves that they had come to reconnoitre the approaches to the North Col, and they attempted by questioning the local inhabitants to determine the source of the Kharta river. The Tibetans, however, knew next to nothing of the high ground overhanging their own valley. A guide then appeared and undertook to lead them to the ' Chomo-Lungma.'

Unfortunately, the man led them off in the wrong direction—to the south—and they finally realized that for him there were two 'Chomo-Lungmas' : the one to which he was leading them was none other than Makalu (27,790 feet)—not Everest, but a neighbouring peak.

This mistake produced one good result : it introduced the mountaineers to one of the most beautiful valleys in the Himalayas —the Khama valley. They found it an enchanting place, with its pastures full of grazing herds, and its brawling streams winding between grassy banks bright with primulas, gentians, and saxifrages. In the clear air the walls of Mt. Makalu, towering majestically in the foreground, gave off a faint bluish glow.

After leaving the valley Mallory and Bullock climbed to the top of a near-by peak in the hope of seeing the eastern face of Everest, and this they managed to do. The face presented a magnificent sight, but seemed terribly liable to ice-falls. They could not see the North Col, however, as it was hidden away in the background. They then returned to Kharta, where Mallory decided to go back up the valley with the object of reaching the col sealing it off at the top—the Lhakpa La or Windy Gap (22,200 feet)—but, as luck would have it, the view was obscured by clouds. All that Mallory could see was the glacier, 1150 feet below him, with its otherwise even surface broken by large crevasses. Once again the North Col had eluded him : would he ever manage to catch sight of it ? Yet he had a strong feeling that it could not be far away, and he was sure enough to be ' ready to bet his bottom dollar ' that the route to the summit lay that way !

So, curbing his impatience, Mallory allowed himself a few days' rest before making his assault. His hopes now ran high ; having settled the question of the route, he could see no reason for not attaining his object—the summit of Everest.

So Mallory made his attack, and this time managed at last to obtain a view of the North Col from the Lhakpa La. It was a formidable barrier of ice, 1640 feet high, and broken by crevasses. It promised to be a tough proposition. Mallory was well aware that all mountain-slopes when seen from the front seem steeper than they really are, but, even when allowances had been made for illusion, this slope promised to be very steep indeed. But as even then it seemed to offer the most likely line of attack, there was no point in hesitating further : an attempt must be made.

Accompanied by Bullock, Wheeler, and a few porters, Mallory set off. The descent of Lhakpa La was completed without a hitch, and the glacier was crossed with the same ease. A camp was set up at 21,000 feet, below the slopes of the North Col. Mallory thought that he had sited his tents in a sheltered position, but they were buffeted all night by strong winds, and nobody had a wink of sleep.

The climb to the North Col turned out to be easier than it had seemed. Apart from one narrow belt of ice, the climbers met with moderately sloping stretches of snow up which they made their way in a wide loop. Only one stage of the climb, near the top, caused anxiety, on account of the steepness of the slope and the doubtful quality of the snow ; later, during the descent, they found that snow had slipped and partially covered their tracks. The uphill climb went off, however, without incident, and by 11.30 A.M. they were on the North Col (22,990 feet).

During the climb Mallory had often looked up at the North Ridge, and what he had seen had gradually confirmed his impression that it was neither dangerous nor difficult.

He was determined to launch his attack there and then. He felt very fit, and above all he was longing to get into action, longing to feel the vast bulk of the enemy beneath his feet.

But once again the wind rose, and as soon as the climbers ventured on to the Col they were hit by a veritable gale. For a while they struggled on, gasping for breath in the gusts of driving wind, while above them the powdery snow on the mountain-side whirled furiously into the air. It was now appallingly cold, and it became obvious that any further advance would be pure folly. The party therefore climbed down again and the whole attempt was called off.

And so, in 1921, mighty Everest emerged untouched from this first encounter with the world of men ; it had taken a mere nothing —a puff of wind—to blow the enemy away.

CHAPTER V

A.J.V.

THE 1922 EXPEDITION

Preliminaries

THE 1921 expedition had determined the route to be followed, and it now remained only to open the final offensive. Success seemed almost certain to every one, and the Tibetan Government were asked to authorize another attempt.

Experience had shown that allowance must be made for casualties within the mountaineering team, owing to the hardships of life at high altitudes, and it was therefore decided that the new team should be larger than its predecessor, and should total thirteen men.

This time Brigadier-General Bruce was available, and he was appointed as expedition leader. He had all the qualities needed for the role—strength of personality, boundless energy, a sense of humour, a cheerful disposition—and he was a born leader into the bargain. Very popular in the Gurkha regiment which he had previously commanded, he liked his men, and was liked by them in return. Finally, he had taken part in a large number of Himalayan expeditions, and had a considerable knowledge of the country and of the inhabitants.

His hand was strengthened by the appointment as second-in-command of Colonel Strutt, an outstanding mountaineer, who was to take charge of operations forward of the base camp.

That year the assault party numbered five : Mallory, Norton, Somervell, Finch, and Wakefield, while other members of the expedition, notably Crawford, Morris, and Morshead, were excellent climbers and could be called in to strengthen the assault party in case of need.

The only members of the expedition who had never climbed before were Noel, the photographer, and Geoffrey Bruce, a young cousin of the General. Longstaff, the Grand Old Man of Himalayan climbers, combined the functions of naturalist and medical officer.

If the lessons of the 1921 expedition were to be applied, it was clear that the expedition must make an earlier start than had been the case the year before. If the previous expedition had in fact suffered little at the hands of the monsoon this was partly because the monsoon had arrived over Everest later than usual, and partly because in the course of the various ascents the different parties had rarely gone higher than 23,000 feet, and it is chiefly at greater heights than this that weather conditions become an important factor.

It was equally important, however, not to start too soon. Winter drags on endlessly on the Tibetan plateau, and in March, for example, the expedition ran the risk of running into dangerous storms while climbing the cols. Such ordeals could not be inflicted upon men of whom every ounce of effort was to be demanded later on. All things considered, it looked as if the expedition ought to get under way early in April, so as to be in the climbing-zone by the 5th or the 10th of May.

Long discussions were held by the Mount Everest Committee as to the advisability of providing the new expedition with oxygen equipment. The diehards made a great fuss in the name of sportsmanship. No mountaineer was worth his salt, they said, if he had to rely on stimulants in order to get to the top. But did that mean that one must condemn a climber for taking a tot of brandy on the mountain-side or for munching a Cola tablet to keep up his

A.J.V.

strength? The argument became heated on either side. Finally the Committee decided to allow the use of oxygen in order to facilitate the opening up of the route which the roped assault party would follow later without masks in the best traditions of fair play.

The approach march followed the same route, more or less, as that inaugurated by Howard-Bury in 1921, but the new expedition found the journey nothing like so enjoyable. In Tibet the winter was barely over ; it was cold, and the rhododendrons were not yet in bloom.

On reaching the Rongbuk monastery Bruce paid a courtesy visit to the Chief Lama, and was much impressed by that dignified, intelligent, and shrewd old gentleman. The Lama for his part honoured his guest by declaring that the General had himself been a Tibetan Lama during a previous incarnation. Judging by the General's horror at the dirtiness of Tibetan monks, he apparently had misgivings regarding that earlier existence of his ! All members of the expedition were struck by the uncleanliness of the Tibetan natives, and used to say that if you *had* to discuss anything with one it was always advisable to stay out in the open and stand well to windward if you didn't want to be asphyxiated !

The Lama inquired as to why the British were anxious to climb Everest. Bruce thereupon had the brilliant idea of telling him that the expedition was carrying out a pilgrimage. They were all members of a sect which worshipped mountains, and it was therefore natural that they should come to worship the highest mountain in the world. This explanation completely satisfied the old monk, who seemed, by the way, not in the least disturbed by the idea that the ascent might disturb the devils who haunt the mountain. He merely warned Bruce against the " Five [Abominable] Snowmen " who are supposed to live in the Rongbuk Glacier.

He also asked the General to see that no animals were killed in the valley. The creatures of the wild are treated with respect by the inhabitants ; as a result they are very friendly, and come regularly to beg for food at the doors of the monastery.

The Lama then brought the conversation to a close by ordering some Tibetan tea. Here Bruce allowed himself one further fib. He stoutly affirmed that he had sworn not to eat butter again until he had reached the top of Everest. The result was that he got a *real* cup of tea—with milk and sugar in it!

The First Attempt

On May 1 an enormous caravan of no less than thirteen climbers, one hundred and fifty porters, and more than three hundred yaks made its way up the Rongbuk valley. The column halted at the foot of the glacier where camp was set up on the moraine's one and only grassy patch, in sight of Everest.

Now that the expedition knew the true course of the East Rongbuk Glacier, it was proposed to take this route to the North Col. As the glacier had never been entirely explored, however, the first step was to make sure that there were no unpleasant surprises in store.

A team led by Strutt went off to reconnoitre ; no obstacles were encountered, and the party made its way among the so-called *nieve penitentes*, and among towers, spires, and pinnacles of ice similar to those which had aroused the admiration of the preceding expedition on the other branches of the glacier.

Camps 1, 2, and 3 were set up in quick succession at intervals of about three hours' march from one another.

A wind of gale force was blowing already, and, seeing Bruce's surprise at this deterioration in the weather just as spring seemed on its way, a porter produced the following explanation. The reason, he said, was that religious services were being held just then at the Rongbuk monastery. These services annoyed the mountain-devils who try to stop them by roaring more loudly than ever. As soon as the services were over the winds would die down. And, in fact, after May 17, the last day of the ceremonies in question, the wind dropped and the weather improved.

On setting out from Camp 3 for the North Col, Mallory was surprised to find that the surface of the slope had altered in the course of the year. As is often the case in the Alps at the end of the cold season, ice had appeared in many places. He was forced to cut steps, drive in wooden pegs, and place fixed ropes in position so as to give some assistance to the porters on the upward journey. It was an enormous task, but nevertheless the North Col was reached and Camp 4 set up in the shelter of a fold in the ice to the north of the dip in the Col itself. The party then went down again and rested.

On May 19 Morshead, Norton, Somervell, and Mallory climbed up in readiness for the first assault. Their aim was to site a fifth camp somewhere on the North Ridge, then to climb as far up as possible, perhaps to the very top. . . .

It was a fine night. " It is always exciting to spend a night under the stars," wrote Mallory. " And such a situation may be arranged quite comfortably ; lying with his head but just within the tent a man has but to stir in his sleep to see, at all events, half the starry sky. Then perhaps thoughts come tumbling from the heavens to slip in at the tent-door ; his dozing is an ecstasy, until, at length, the alarm-watch sounds ; and after . . . ? " [1]

Afterwards it was all that Mallory could do to get the porters up—they had shut themselves up so snugly in their tents that they had cut their air-supply off, and were in the first stages of asphyxia,

[1] See C. K. Howard-Bury, *Mount Everest : The Reconnaissance, 1921*, p. 228.

suffering from terrible headaches as a result. The fact is that high-altitude tents are especially designed to be completely waterproof. The walls are sewn to the ground-sheet, so that when your tent is pitched you find yourself in a sort of container, which is completely air-tight except for the entrance flap—so it is a good thing to keep the latter open !

In the Himalayas climbers do not set off at first light as they do in the Alps ; owing to the cold the start has to be delayed until the sun is up. That morning, unfortunately, the party were denied the warmth of the sun's rays, and they shivered with cold as they cooked their breakfast, struggling with tins of spaghetti in tomato sauce frozen so hard that not even ice-axes made any impression !

By 7.30 they were on their way, and half an hour later they had reached the col, where they had a good look at the enemy's defences. The rounded and blunted North Ridge seemed to offer a safe and inviting means of approach, which Mallory compared to the easiest section of the Hörnli ridge on the Matterhorn.

As Morshead seemed in better shape than the rest, he was asked to take the lead, and thus had the honour of being the first man to set foot on the mountain !

He decided to climb via a belt of rocky ground on which the stones had been frozen into place ; these were flat enough to form rough stepping-stones. No terrain could have been more suitable. All went well to begin with, as the air was still, but soon the merciless Tibetan winds rose in their fury. The cold became intense, and the sky became filmed over with a mist which blotted out all radiation from the sun.

The climbers stopped to put on extra clothing. Unfortunately for them the ' anorak,' with its comfortable, close-fitting hood, was still unknown, and they had only Balaclava helmets and felt hats. They also wore puttees wrapped tightly round their stockings : they were warm and ' supported the calves,' as the saying was, but they also hindered the circulation.

On again they plodded, leaning forward, battling with the gusts of wind and fighting for breath as they went. At every step it seemed as though their lungs would burst. Soon the cold attacked their fingers, toes, and ears.

Mallory had taken over the lead and was trying to reach the slope of the ridge away from the wind. He kept cutting steps in the hard snow, and, although he was using both hands, found it exhausting work.

At 11.30, by mutual agreement, the climbers decided that it was time to look for a camping-place, as the porters were to go down again before nightfall : it proved very difficult to find a suitable spot.

Although the North Ridge is not very steep, it has no level surfaces. The strata run in such a way that the layers of rock overlap one another like tiles on a roof and slope downward towards empty space. In sheer despair of finding a better place two separate sites were chosen, and made suitable by building platforms

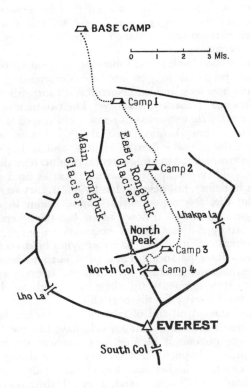

The 1922 Expedition : the Approach from the North

with stones. It was heavy work, for the mere effort to bend down made a man pant for breath.

By about 3 P.M. the tents were up, the porters had left on the downward journey, and the 'sahibs' were on their own. A meal was prepared and quickly eaten, every one being anxious to get into the warmth of the eiderdown sleeping-bags.

Getting into bed under canvas at high altitudes is an operation demanding a certain amount of thought. First of all, there is the problem of *boots*. They simply *must* be protected from cold if one does not want the job of thawing them out next day over the flame of a spirit-stove or candle.

Some get into their sleeping-bag with their boots on. Others take them off and slip them into the bottom of the bag—a poor sort of hot-water-bottle ! Mallory put his into his rucksack, which he then used as a pillow ; he claimed that he always found his boots warm next morning, even if he *did* get called a hot-head ! He also advised the others to place their pillows as high as possible as an aid to breathing.

He got into ' bed,' and found a more or less comfortable position ; then Norton prepared to get into the sleeping-bag with him. " Considering how long and thin Norton is it's surprising how much room he takes up," remarked Mallory. The two men were jammed together so closely that whenever one of them stirred the other had to move too. Stones bruised their shoulder-blades through the ground-sheet, they found it hard to breathe, and as they got warmer they became aware of the tingling soreness produced by slight touches of frost-bite. They got up next morning just as tired as they had been the night before, but nevertheless by 8 A.M. they were off again.

After the first few rope-lengths fatigue began to take effect. Morshead gave up and went down again, but the others continued. Fortunately, they did not find it necessary to secure handholds and pull themselves up : they had merely to hold on the rock in order to keep their balance. They tried hard to breathe rhythmically, inhaling and exhaling several times at every step. Every twenty yards they stopped to fill their lungs with air, building up a little reserve of energy for the next effort.

They had started off full of false notions. They had thought they could reach the summit in a single day, but the farther they went the more obvious it became that this was impossible. But on they went. So hypnotized were they by the thought that they must keep climbing higher and higher, and still keep climbing, that they simply didn't stop. And, after all, time spent in reconnaissance is seldom wasted.

At 2.15 P.M. they came to a standstill. It had become clear that if they were to reach the North Col again before nightfall it was time to start getting down.

They tried to take nourishment, but found it hard to swallow their dried fruit, mint-cake, and chocolate. They were suffering severely from thirst, and not a trickle of water was to be seen on the rocks, temperatures on Everest being too low for the snow to melt. Munching away in disgust, they looked down at the landscape. Behind them the summit of Everest seemed surprisingly close ; the neighbouring mountains lay below them, and only then did they realize how high they had reached. They had in fact climbed to 26,986 feet, a height never previously attained.

On the way down they picked up Morshead as they passed Camp 5. The snow that had fallen during the night still covered the slabs and made them slippery. They were tired, climbing down with difficulty, and no longer very sure of their movements. It is always at times like these that the mountains catch you unawares.

The whole roped party were crossing a snow-covered slope when Mallory, in the lead, heard an unusual sound behind him, and turned round. His three companions had slipped, snatching one another away from the steps cut in the snow. Quickly he drove his ice-axe into the snow, threw the rope around it, and pulled with all his might. Experience has shown that it is impossible for one man to hold three others ; either he is pulled away in his turn or else the rope snaps. Barring a miracle, that is, and miracles sometimes happen. The second man on the rope had no doubt been caught by a rock ; held for a moment, he had checked his companions' fall, and thus prevented the weight of three men from bearing at once on the rope. Despite the severe strain suddenly imposed on it, the rope had held, thus averting an accident.

After this narrow escape the four men were more careful, which meant that the pace became slower than ever. As a result darkness had fallen by the time they reached the North Col ; and that windswept threshold of Everest had still to be crossed. They lit a lantern, but lost their way, traversing right and left among the crevasses and jumping over walls of ice. While they were desperately searching for the fixed rope which they had rigged up on the last steep slope their light went out for good. When finally they reached Camp 4 at 11 P.M. they were groping in the dark and tottering on their feet.

They were in desperate need of something to drink, for laboured breathing had dried their throats, and the rapid evaporation present at great heights had drawn the moisture from their bodies. They were preparing to melt some snow when they discovered that the porters had taken all the utensils away with them by mistake. Catastrophe was complete. They slipped into their sleeping-bags, utterly exhausted.

During the last stages of the descent Mallory had kept confusing Morshead with Longstaff, and despite the former's protests had persistently called him by the other man's name. Yet in his mind the two men remained quite distinct, and he knew perfectly well that it was Longstaff who wore a beard and not Morshead. Nevertheless, he persisted in his error until the following morning.

The First Use of Oxygen

As Finch was a lecturer in chemistry he had been placed in charge of the oxygen equipment. No sooner had he unpacked the breathing appliances at Base Camp than he found them in urgent need of repair ; the jolting incurred on the way up had done them no good, and they were leaking in every direction. They had, however, been specially designed for the expedition and with mountaineering requirements in view. Hitherto airmen alone had used oxygen at high altitudes.

Each individual outfit weighed 30 lb. in all, and consisted of a frame worn on the back and carrying four steel cylinders charged with compressed oxygen. The oxygen was led along copper tubes into an apparatus worn on the chest and fitted with pressure-gauges. From here it passed through a rubber tube into a mask covering the climber's nose and mouth. Unfortunately, the mask had serious disadvantages : it made breathing unbearably difficult while climbing, and became covered with moisture which then froze solid.

Finch was fortunately a first-class handyman. Using pieces of glass tubing and football bladders, and working away for days with hacksaw, pliers, and soldering-iron, he altered the masks and made them suitable for use in the mountains. It was a praiseworthy achievement on Finch's part, for the work had all to be done in the open air, and the atmosphere was so cold, in spite of the sun, that the metal tools frequently stuck to his fingers.

As soon as the equipment was ready Finch carried out one or two trials. These proved satisfactory, and he reported that he was ready to make a start.

More by chance than anything else, Finch found himself teamed up with Geoffrey Bruce and a Gurkha porter, both somewhat inexperienced, perhaps, but far from lacking the necessary qualities. Geoffrey Bruce had never climbed before, but he was a first-class athlete, while the Gurkha was the best of the native climbers—what more could one ask ? Both were novices, however, which meant that Finch must take full responsibility for the climb. He alone would be in a position to judge of the seriousness of any situation, and he would have to rely on his own initiative.

On the morning of May 25 he sent his porters forward from the North Col with the necessary gear to set up the high-altitude camp. An hour and a half later he and his companions set out, wearing their oxygen equipment, and during the climb had the satisfaction of overtaking and passing the column of porters.

At a height of about 25,500 feet Finch called a halt, a platform

Mallory and Norton

was levelled off, and the tent pitched. The porters then went down, singing the songs of their native hills.

The wind had already risen, and snow had been falling for some time. Now it began to snow in earnest, and the wind rose to gale force ; it became very cold. The three men lost no time in putting on extra clothing, and took refuge in their tent. They tried making hot drinks to warm themselves up, but the best they could produce was lukewarm tea. At great heights water boils at such low temperatures that it is possible to dip the finger-tips in it without any risk of being scalded.

From sunset onward the gale turned into a hurricane, and the position became critical, the small tent being unprotected by any natural cover. It was assailed by gusts of such violence that at times the wind got under the ground-sheet, lifting it and its human burden. Once the wind got hold of the tent both it and its occupants would roll down into the depths of the Rongbuk Glacier. The three men clung to the masts and fought for dear life. The canvas flapped with the rattle of a machine-gun, and the tent-doors bellied in the wind and threatened to split asunder. Guy-ropes were swept away and were rapidly repaired whenever the wind slackened ; the tent was likewise made fast by means of the climbing-rope. These sorties into the ice-cold wind lasted three or four minutes at most, but were enough to deprive the men of what little warmth remained in their bodies, and left them shivering for long periods in their sleeping-bags. They found it impossible to protect themselves against the snow, which filtered invisibly into everything ; they were covered with snow, and it had even got into their clothes !

At dawn the wind was still as violent as ever, but the snow had stopped falling. The three men took the opportunity to slip out and hastily build a protective wall.

They tried to cook some food, but the flickering flame of their spirit-stove threatened to set the tent on fire ; the latter was damaged already, a stone loosened by the wind having fallen upon it, making a hole in the fabric and giving the wind something to tear at.

Towards 1 P.M. the pressure diminished and the storm slackened off. Anyone else would have immediately seized the opportunity to go back down, but Finch was stubborn. He had come to ' have a go,' and have a go he would ! With some anxiety he asked his companions what they thought of it, and to his intense satisfaction found that Bruce had lost nothing of his enthusiasm, while the Gurkha's face lit up in a broad and confident grin.

Unfortunately, there was more than the weather to worry about ; there was also the question of food and fuel. Only one day's allowance of each had been carried, and now supplies were running low. They must obviously ration themselves strictly, and the result was a gloomy meal.

They prepared to seek forgetfulness in sleep, and were just settling into their sleeping-bags when, to their astonishment, voices were heard outside—not the voices of mountain-devils, but friendly voices, the voices of a team of porters.

Setting a wonderful—and characteristic—example of devoted loyalty, the stout fellows had come up of their own accord from the North Col as soon as the storm had abated. They had come to see how the climbers were faring, and to bring them help. This included Thermos-flasks full of broth and steaming tea which were much appreciated.

The porters were expecting the mountaineers to go down with them, for no climbing team had hitherto dared to spend two consecutive nights at a high altitude. They were therefore taken aback when Finch thanked them warmly and sent them away.

As the sun began to set the three men shut themselves up in their tent for the second time. The night promised to be an uncomfortable one, for they were worn out by their struggle with the storm, by lack of sleep and food. Gradually Bruce's expression became grim and set, the smile disappeared from the Gurkha's face, and Finch felt his legs growing numb in the deadly cold. The situation was becoming grave. Then Finch had the idea of taking a whiff of oxygen. The result was miraculous : warmth and life returned instantaneously to his deadened limbs. Bruce and the Gurkha took a few whiffs of gas, too, with the result that Bruce relaxed and the Gurkha recovered his smile. They immediately arranged things so as to be able to breathe small quantities of oxygen during the night, and as a result they felt warm and slept soundly. Every time Bruce let the mouthpiece slip from between his lips as he slept he unconsciously tossed and turned until he found it. Then he would calm down again, like a baby when it gets the teat of the bottle back into its mouth.

The climbers unfortunately had no substitute for food, and by morning they felt weak for want of nourishment. By 6.30, however, they were on their way.

The weather was clear and the wind had dropped to a tolerable if ice-cold breeze. Progress was slow. Suddenly, at about 26,000 feet, the Gurkha collapsed, completely exhausted. His companions relieved him of one or two oxygen cylinders, and then sent him back to Camp 5. He was able to get down alone, the tent being in sight and the track presenting no difficulty.

The two Britishers went on. The going must have been easy,

D

since Finch did not consider it necessary to rope up despite the
fact that Bruce was a novice—climbing, in fact, for the first time in
his life !

At intervals the climbers stopped to change an oxygen cylinder,
throwing the empty one away and listening with satisfaction 'as it
went down, bouncing from rock to rock with the sound of a clanging
bell. "Five pounds less to carry," was the one thought in their
minds.

The wind had now strengthened, and Finch was forced to leave
the ridge and climb up the North Face, which was less exposed to

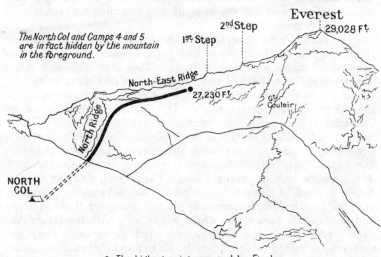

The North Col and Camps 4 and 5 are in fact hidden by the mountain in the foreground.

Everest
29,028 Ft.
2nd Step
1st Step
North-East Ridge
27,230 Ft.
Gt. Couloir
North Ridge
NORTH COL

● The highest point reached by Finch

squalls. He made this decision with some regret, for the rocks on
the ridge had been swept clean by the wind, and the ground itself
presented no difficulties.

As soon as they had reached the North Face the two men
ran into trouble. The slope was steeper, with occasional stretches
of treacherous, powdery snow covered by a thin, frozen crust.

Finch's object was to get back on to the ridge, somewhere
between the shoulder and the summit of Everest, but suddenly a
technical hitch occurred and Bruce's oxygen apparatus jammed.
Finch had to go down to him and connect his own apparatus to
Bruce's mask while he carried out the necessary repairs.

There seems little doubt that Finch must have managed to
resist that mental numbness and that sapping of the will which

generally overtake human beings at great heights, for he not only found out what was wrong with Bruce's equipment but had enough determination to put it right. In all likelihood it was owing to oxygen that he managed to regain control of all his faculties.

Had the two men not halted they would presumably have gone on climbing for some time, but now that they had stopped they suddenly felt extremely tired. It was midday, and they realized that it was too late to reach the top of Everest and get back before nightfall, so they decided to beat a retreat. But before setting off again Bruce looked up at " the one and only still undefeated Goddess Mother of the World " and delivered this challenge as his parting shot : " Just you wait, old thing, you'll be for it soon ! "

They were to learn later that they had beaten Mallory's record, having reached a height of more than 27,300 feet.

Meanwhile they roped up and hurriedly prepared to climb down as the weather had taken a turn for the worse, with the ragged shapes of large clouds surrounding them on all sides. In half an hour they reached Camp 5, where they found the Gurkha sleeping, rolled in the three sleeping-bags. Some porters could be seen making their way up, so Finch and Bruce left it to them to bring their team-mate back to camp while they themselves went on down. They felt weak at the knees, and their legs kept giving way beneath them, but they still managed to keep up a good enough pace to reach the North Col by 4 P.M. They took a quick snack and pressed on, reaching Camp 3 forty minutes later.

There they really let themselves go. Four truffled quails smothered in *pâté de foie gras* and nine sausages failed to satisfy Finch's hunger, and he fell asleep with the remains of a tin of biscuits in his arms !

The Avalanche on the North Col

The unsettled state of the weather now gave grim warning of the approaching monsoon. Every morning from 9 or 10 A.M. onward the sky became overcast and Everest disappeared behind the clouds, reappearing only in the evening. It was the period of the year during which the winds unleash all their fury, before starting to blow in the reverse direction.

Mallory, Crawford, and Somervell were moving up from the Base Camp with a long procession of porters. Snow was falling, wet and sticky snow, and they did not feel very optimistic as they floundered along. On arriving at Camp 3 they were met by a dismal sight : the tents had been struck as a precautionary measure,

A.J.V.

and both tents and stores were now hidden under a foot and a half of snow. Picks had to be used to get them out.

That evening the mountaineers talked things over in their tent. Was it wise to carry on? The risk of avalanches promised to be serious on the way up to the North Col, and the snow seemed likely to shift, not only on the final slope but on the first one, which until then had been covered with ice. . . .

Our present knowledge of Himalayan snow has taken many years to acquire. It differs considerably from that of the Alps, in that above a certain height, as a result of permanently low temperatures, it does not go through that alternation of frost and thaw which might otherwise give it solidity and depth. Either it remains powdery or else it forms a crust under the pressure of the wind. Mallory and his companions were not, as far as we know, ski-ing enthusiasts. Had that been the case, they might well have been better prepared for the unpleasant surprises which the snow so often has in store, even in the Himalayas. There is no doubt that, under winter conditions, skiers get more opportunities of studying snow than climbers do in the mountains during the summer. The British, no doubt for geographical reasons, have always been climbers rather than ski-ing men. It is true, however, that in 1922 there were few Alpine skiers about, even in mountainous countries.

Mallory and his companions were anxious because, although they had only slight knowledge of the slopes on the North Col, they knew how dangerous they might be. Yet if they were to succeed they must take the risks involved ; since no other route was possible, they had no choice. They were willing to accept a certain element of risk—Everest being no place for family outings— but their problem was to estimate the *degree* of risk which they could reasonably take. Hence their hesitation. Mallory had not forgotten the warning he had had from the slopes of the North Col a year before in the course of his first attempt.

On the day following this discussion the weather was fine and relatively warm. As a result of the warm monsoon winds the stones of the moraine were visible and around the camp the snow was becoming firm and compact. High up on Everest the wind was sweeping the North Ridge clear ; such a fine opportunity could not be allowed to go by.

Following upon the performance of Finch's team, it was decided to use oxygen equipment on the next attempt, at least from the high-altitude camp onward. This meant extra weight, not counting the burden of extra rations ; for oxygen stimulates appetite, and extra weight meant extra transport. So a large party was organized, including no less than fourteen porters.

At 8 A.M. on June 7 the roped parties moved off. They took two hours to reach the snowfields leading to the lower slopes of the North Col. In spite of overnight frost the snow failed to hold; the crust kept breaking, the leaders sank in knee-deep, and had to take it in turns to break the trail. On the first steep slope they tested the snow by deliberately breaking the surface ; the snow held, and they moved on with more confidence. The going was hard, and halts were unavoidably frequent.

Towards 1 P.M. they were approaching the final slope, nevertheless the stretch of snow which they were crossing was not particularly steep. Close behind one another, they moved up in a silence broken only by the sound of laboured breathing. Suddenly a dull, muffled, tearing noise broke the silence. Mallory had never heard anything like it before, but he knew at once what it meant. An avalanche ! A hundred feet higher up the snow had broken away ; now all around them it was cracking, splitting, and forming into folds. Then the whole layer went down bodily, carrying them with it.

Flat on his back, Mallory fought to stop himself slipping round head-downward. At first he slid down slowly with the moving snow, but soon the pace quickened. He felt the rope jerk, and immediately a mass of snow broke over him like a wave. Then he remembered what the books tell one to do in such cases, and started ' swimming ' on his back. Completely buried, he could see nothing and had lost all sense of speed, but realized from the increasing pressure of the snow surrounding his body that the pace was slackening, and the agonizing question arose in his mind: how long would it be before he stifled to death? Then the avalanche stopped.

By sheer chance his arms were free and his legs were close to the surface; after a short struggle he got to his feet, panting for breath. He then saw that the rope attached to his belt led down into the snow; it was the rope connecting him to one of the porters. He gave it a pull, and to his astonishment out came the porter, safe and sound. A little farther on Somervell and Crawford struggled free in their turn. Where were the rest? A hundred and fifty feet below them four porters stood motionless, as if turned to stone; they were pointing to something below them. The climbers hurried down and found themselves on the edge of a sheer drop of about fifty feet. Then they realized what had happened: the nine missing men had shot over the edge with the avalanche, falling into the crevasse where the enormous mass of snow had buried them. Quickly they made their way round the crevasse and with the help of the porters began feverishly digging, using ice-axes and bare hands. It was hard, slow work, as the heaped-up snow had become compact and hard.

Two men only were recovered and brought back to life. The seven others were dead.

That year the proud mountain had met the human invader with the full force of its wrath. Their attack had been savagely repelled, and now it was war to the knife.

A.J.V.

R.J.V.

CHAPTER VI

THE 1924 EXPEDITION

The Lessons of 1921 and 1922

THANKS to the first two expeditions, scientists had obtained some useful information as to the presence of wild life at high altitudes, animals having been found at considerable heights. Wolves had been seen at 19,000 feet and a fox, a hare, and a bharal, or wild sheep, at over 20,000 feet. At the latter height a mouse had got into the tent and had nibbled at the rations ; no one, however, had actually managed to catch sight of it. Birds, of course, flew up to great heights. The lammergeier reached nearly 25,000 feet, and the jackdaw more than 26,200, although even for them such heights were exceptional.

The highest living creature in the world—living on the ground, that is, as opposed to birds—seemed to be a small, black, short-legged spider of the Attides family. It was found living at heights of 22,000 feet, under stones and loose rocks. What it lived on was a mystery, for at such heights no other sign of organic life was to be seen. Perhaps it simply waited for the odd butterfly, blown off its course and wafted upward by the wind.

It had been shown that human beings could live at nearly 27,000 feet, a fact regarding which there had previously been some doubt. It was now known, too, that man was capable of ac-climatization, and that in the course of a second climb to a high altitude he stood up better to the test. If he stayed, however, above 23,000 feet he gradually weakened, and a kind of deterioration set in.

It was now understood that it was impossible to reach the summit of Everest direct from Camp 5, as climbers moved too slowly at heights above 26,000 feet. It was therefore essential to set up an intermediary Camp 6 so as to shorten the final stage.

The two-men assault team was now recognized to be the best, since it was the fastest, and it was considered advisable to ' double-up ' with a support party of two, capable of holding a watching brief over the first team, assisting them if necessary and taking care of them on their return. In 1921 Mallory's party had had to endure additional hardships because, as a result of an error in organization, the camp on the North Col had turned out to be deserted when they reached it, worn out, at 11 P.M.

The oxygen question, too, had been raised all over again. There had always been some, of course, who were against it. The astonishing results obtained by Finch's team, however, were gradually tipping the balance in favour of its use. The facts were that after spending two nights at Camp 5 they had succeeded in climbing over 300 feet higher than the preceding team, moving up at the rate of nearly 1000 feet per hour as compared with their 360 feet. Lastly, on the return journey, they had gone straight down to Camp 3, arriving towards 5 P.M., while Mallory's team had only reached Camp 4 by 11 P.M.

The group of climbers who prepared to set out in the spring of 1924 included several well-known Himalayan mountaineers— General Bruce, Somervell, Mallory, and Geoffrey Bruce. There had been some hesitation about inviting Mallory, as he was now married, but when sounded as to his feelings he had expressed a strong desire to take part. As for Geoffrey Bruce, his appetite had been whetted by an exceptional *début*, and he had taken part in a number of climbs in Switzerland during the summer of 1923.

The newcomers were as follows : Odell, Beetham, Hazard— all experienced mountaineers—Shebbeare, Hingston, and Irvine. The latter, a tall, handsome fellow of twenty-two, was the youngest member of the team : he had never climbed before, but was an athlete and a ski-ing enthusiast who had already shown up well during an expedition to Spitzbergen. He was considered to be a worthy substitute for Finch, since like the latter he was remarkably clever with his hands.

When the question of hiring porters arose it was feared that the 1922 catastrophe might have left the Sherpas with such dreadful memories that recruiting would be seriously affected, but this was not the case. When the time arrived porters came forward to join at Darjeeling in greater numbers than ever.

On the morning following the accident the reactions of the survivors, amounting to a sort of fatalistic resignation, had caused surprise. The reason was simply that, to men brought up to look upon the body as a sort of garment to be exchanged one day for another, death is neither final nor frightening ; to them it is only a brief interlude. If men had been killed it meant that their turn had come ; if it was written that *they* too were to die on Everest, then they would die ; if it was written that they were not to, then they would *not* die, for man is in the hands of the gods !

Preliminary Skirmishes

From the moment the expedition arrived at the Base Camp the struggle with Everest began afresh ; this year it was the mountain which attacked from the outset, deploying its old allies—wind, frost, and snow—against the invader. Despite a battering from the gale, the caravans moved up on to the Rongbuk Glacier, butting their way forward into the wind.

After a long series of advances and strategic retreats, Camps 1, 2, and 3 were set up on the usual sites.

A blizzard was raging, and snow found its way into everything. It was appallingly cold, and a number of men fell seriously ill ; there were cases of frost-bite, throat trouble, and even pneumonia among the expedition. As a result it was decided to make a temporary withdrawal to Base Camp. On the way down a Gurkha died of thrombosis, and one of the Sherpas, with his feet frost-bitten up to the ankles, died shortly after reaching camp. The porters' morale was now badly affected, and they had lost all semblance of enthusiasm. They had endured too much, and it was essential to build up their determination again before calling upon them for a further effort. The expedition therefore went down to the Rongbuk monastery and received the Chief Lama's blessing in the course of a solemn religious ceremony. Europeans and natives one by one approached the holy man, who touched each of them on the head with a small prayer-wheel. Then, in a short address to the porters, he called upon them to persevere, and assured them that he would pray on their behalf. The simple, stout-hearted Sherpas returned from the service comforted in spirit.

Unfortunately, the withdrawal had wasted much precious time, the days were slipping by and the monsoon was on its way. . . . Conditions were so bad that the fresh attack had to be postponed again and again. It was now the turn of the British to lose something

of their morale. " I look back on a tremendous effort and
exhaustion and dismal looking out of a tent door into a world of
snow and vanishing hopes," wrote Mallory to his wife.[1]

As soon as the weather improved he set out for the North Col
with Norton, Odell, and one porter, and was disagreeably surprised
to find on the way up that the relief of the slope had altered during
the previous two years. Half-way up there was now a crescent-
shaped crevasse about a quarter of a mile long. It was impossible
to get round the crevasse ; it would have to be crossed.

With the help of his companion, who supported his foot with
the head of an ice-axe, Mallory proceeded to cut steps in the vertical
ice-wall and then slipped into a narrow chimney, the walls of
which were quite smooth and touched with blue reflections. He
then had to perform a horrible series of gymnastic feats which left
him panting for breath. Next came the steepest and most dangerous
slope of the whole ascent. Tired out as he was by his efforts,
Mallory insisted on remaining in the lead and continued up the
sheer wall, ramming the snow firm, cutting steps in the ice, and
traversing wherever the slope became more manageable. All went
well, and they reached the North Col.

However, the valiant Mallory still felt that he had not yet done
enough, and he was anxious to reconnoitre the ground separating
the terrace, on which camp was to be pitched, from the Col
itself. It was a maze of crevasses and snow-ridges, and had two
years earlier forced the climbing parties returning from the North
Ridge to make numerous detours. With an effort the four men
tore themselves away from the luxury of a halt in the sunshine and
went on.

Unfortunately, they were weary with fatigue, and had lost their
usual sureness of touch. Suddenly Norton slipped, followed by the
porter ; luckily they managed to hang on, but Mallory then broke
through a snow-bridge and fell ten feet into a crevasse ; as he was
not roped to the others they did not notice that he had disappeared.
His shouts went unheard, and no one came to his aid. Hanging
by one hand from his ice-axe, which had fortunately caught across
the top of the crevasse, Mallory was left squirming above a black
hole for several dreadful moments before climbing back up to the
light of day.

The approach to the Col had now been mapped out, and Camp
4 was set up. Immediately the weather changed for the worse,
and soon it was appallingly bad, with snow continuing for the next
thirty-six hours.

[1] *The Fight for Everest : 1924*, by Lieutenant-Colonel E. F. Norton and other
members of the expedition (Arnold, 1925), p. 236.

Several roped parties went down, but soon there was anxiety at Camp 3 as to the four porters left alone at the North Col. Without the moral support of the white men they would soon be tormented by superstitious fears. They were to declare later, in fact, that all night long they had heard the barking of the dogs guarding the throne of the Goddess herself! The fact that two of the men were suffering from frost-bite was particularly worrying, and there was nothing for it but to go and bring them down without delay.

Mallory, Somervell, and Norton, although suffering them-

A.J.V.

selves from rheumatism, throat trouble, and extreme fatigue, accepted the responsibility and struggled up through deep snow which threatened to come away in an avalanche at any moment. On reaching the last slope they caught sight of one of the Sherpas on the edge of the terrace at the top, and shouted, " Are you fit enough to walk ? " " Up or down ? " cried the Sherpa. " Down, you idiot ! " was the reply. Thereupon the Sherpa disappeared in a flash and returned with his three comrades.

Somervell, watched anxiously by Mallory and Norton, climbed up towards them ; frequently his cough overcame him and forced him to stop, but at last he had run out the full length of the rope. The Sherpas were now a few yards away. Somervell encouraged them to come down towards him ; the first two reached him without difficulty and grasped the rope which he was holding out to support them. It was a different story with the remaining pair ; through over-anxiety they started down together, moving a layer of snow which began to slip down with them. . . . Down they came, flat on their backs, but as though by a miracle the snow stopped of its own accord a little farther on. The rescue party shouted to them to sit down and keep still, which they did, trembling in every limb. Somervell then moved towards them. He had unfastened himself from the rope, and was holding it at arm's length so as not to waste an inch of its length. He stretched, reached out, took hold of one man, pulled him in until he was within the ' anchorage ' of Somervell's ice-axe, and repeated the procedure with the second. From then on the two unfortunates, badly shaken by the incident, were no longer capable of walking properly. They kept slipping and breaking the steps cut in the surface, and were held back only by the solid grip of the Englishmen on the rope in their rear.

Now that we know what the future held in store, one cannot help feeling that the mountain was doing its best in these various incidents to discourage the invaders, convince them of the folly of further effort, and persuade them to go. If only they had taken the lesson to heart . . .

The Highest Man of the Year

Time was now pressing, for the monsoon was close at hand. The climbers talked things over, and it was decided, in view of the casualties among the porters, to lighten their loads by making the next attempt without oxygen.

On June 1, in fine weather, a party led by Mallory and Geoffrey Bruce moved off to set up Camp 5 at nearly 25,000 feet on the North Ridge. On the way up they had to force their way through such a bitter wind that the porters were soon exhausted ; Bruce had to assist the last two men, going back to bring them up and carrying their loads himself, for by now they could no longer walk. Next day the exhausted men refused to move on and establish

Camp 6. They were all ' tigers '—*i.e.*, porters picked from the very best of the Sherpas—and Bruce, who spoke their language fluently, could normally get his way with them, but now they were at the end of their tether. The attempt was therefore called off, and the party went down again. On the ridge they met Norton and Somervell with their team, making their way up.

They in their turn had suffered from the cold as soon as they had left Camp 4. On reaching the North Col they had lost sight of the sun for some time and had met the full fury of the Tibetan wind. It took their breath away like a plunge into ice-cold water. In a couple of minutes, despite their gloves, they lost all feeling in their hands and had difficulty in hanging on to the frozen rocks for support against the driving squalls.

They were wearing good protective clothing—woollen vest, woollen shirt, two pullovers, gabardine jacket, and wind-proof outer covering, but there are winds capable of piercing the strongest wind-jackets, and some kinds of rain that no waterproof can ever keep out. Norton was wearing a leather, fur-lined motor-cyclist's helmet, and his nose and eyes were protected by glasses sewn into a leather mask covering the parts of his face not already protected by his beard. In spite of everything he complained like every one else of feeling naked and defenceless against that bitter, lashing wind. The gusts reached such violence that the porters literally rocked on their feet.

Norton and Somervell had no difficulty in finding Camp 5, thanks to the strips of coloured cloth which Mallory and Bruce, like Tom Thumb, had left behind to mark the track.

Next day they had endless trouble in getting the porters on to their feet. For nearly four hours they argued with them, encouraging them, trying to revive their enthusiasm, telling them what glory and honour would be theirs if they managed to push on beyond the highest point to which a load had ever been carried. These arguments had little effect on the porters, poor devils ; they had had enough. Finally, however, they made up their minds, picked up their loads, and started to climb.

Camp 6 was set up at 26,800 feet—a magnificent achievement—after which the porters went down, leaving the two Englishmen alone.

Next day, after a fairly restful night, in spite of the altitude, and the fact that a Thermos-flask had decided to empty itself into one of the sleeping-bags, Norton and Somervell moved off at six-thirty. They were not roped together.

After climbing for an hour, they reached the great ' Yellow Band,' one of the features of the northern face of Everest and visible from a great distance, running parallel to the final ridge but 500 feet below it. They were now on virgin ground, no previous climber having ever got so far. It was an inspiring thought, and for a time their ardour quickened.

They certainly needed encouragement, for the going was fearfully hard, and progress pitifully slow. They started counting their steps. Norton aimed at maintaining twenty steps between halts, but each time he reached thirteen he had to stop for a ' breather,' and rest his elbow on his knee. Somervell, whose throat was already giving him trouble, was constantly held up by fits of coughing. One can well imagine the disastrous effect which the ice-cold air and rapid breathing must have had on his already irritated windpipe.

Nevertheless, they both went on. Crossing the Yellow Band, they found the terrain less difficult, as it formed a series of broken ledges.

As they climbed they tried to forget their difficulties by looking at the scenery, but found it disappointing. From lower down the great snowy peaks and the glaciers with moraines running parallel to one another like cartwheel ruts in the snow, were an impressive sight, but now they seemed flattened out ; their appearance was blurred and their beauty of line was gone.

Still the two men went on. Norton was beginning to have trouble with his vision ; he was beginning to ' see double,' finding it difficult to place his feet accurately. This made him anxious, as he feared it might be an early sign of snow-blindness.

Towards midday the climbers found themselves on the upper edge of the Yellow Band, not far from the Great Couloir. This falls away vertically from the Ridge to the east of the ' pyramid ' forming the summit itself.

At this point Somervell gave up, overcome by throat trouble, but he insisted that Norton should go on alone, and sat down to wait for him. Had he gone down he would have suffered less from cold, but he preferred to stay where he was, keep an eye on his companion, and give him a helping hand on the way down if necessary.

Norton started off again, to fight his lonely battle, all alone now in this final grapple with the mountain. Without a friend beside him he would be more vulnerable, more accessible to discouragement and fear. Cowardice comes easily to those alone at great heights, and this was the highest mountain in the world. . . . But Norton pressed on regardless, a tiny black point in an immense waste of rocks and snow. He was now close to the Great Couloir itself ; thereafter the ground became much more difficult. The slope became steeper and the winding ' track ' narrowed and then broke up into mere handholds and footholds a few inches in breadth. Norton moved carefully upward. In the Couloir he met thick and powdery snow, sinking into it knee-deep and even up to his waist. He was on dangerous ground, but continued to move upward. On the other side of the Couloir the smooth rocks, sloping downward into space, would offer little purchase to his nailed boots. The slightest movement had to be made with the greatest care. He felt his nerves tighten, and his eye-strain immediately returned. He halted.

He estimated that he had about sixty-five yards of difficult rock to climb before reaching the base of the final ' pyramid ' where

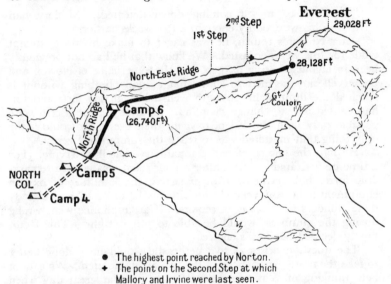

● The highest point reached by Norton.
✦ The point on the Second Step at which Mallory and Irvine were last seen.

the angle of the slope altered. It was already 1 P.M., and at his present rate of progress there was not enough time to climb the 300 to 350 yards separating him from the summit. He therefore decided to go back. He had reached a height of 28,128 feet, a record which was to remain unbeaten for many years (see map above).

Imagination readily conjures up a picture of Norton, bitterly disappointed at having to admit defeat so close to his goal, but in fact he felt nothing but immense relief at the thought that the ordeal was over. One of the worst effects of great heights is to sap the climber's determination to succeed.

Slowly he retraced his steps, but his nerves had undergone too great a strain. As he was about to rejoin Somervell fear overcame him at the thought of crossing a particular stretch of snow alone.

It was neither steep nor difficult, and he had easily negotiated it on the upward journey. This time he had to get his partner to throw a rope out to him.

The two men went down, arriving by nightfall at the North Col. Next day Norton began to suffer from an inflammation of the eyes as a result of having occasionally taken off his snow-glasses. These glasses are indispensable on Everest, even on rock, owing to the glare of the sun's rays.

Their Last Attempt

" I can't see myself coming down defeated," Mallory had written to his wife, oddly enough, a few weeks earlier.

After Norton's return, he was eager to make his own attempt while the fine weather lasted. We know that he had not previously been in favour of using oxygen, but the experience of Norton and Somervell now seemed to show that a man climbing without it reached the limit of his strength well below 28,900 feet, and this had caused him to change his mind. If, after all, the ascent were possible only with the aid of oxygen, then use it he would ; the only thing that mattered was to reach the summit of Everest.

He had the choice of two companions—Odell or Irvine. For a time he hesitated : Odell, after a poor start, was now in remark-able form, but Irvine was an expert in the handling of oxygen equipment ; he was very clever with his hands, and had already done wonders in the way of repairs. If an appliance went wrong during the climb he would be able to put it right. This factor finally decided Mallory's choice.

The question arises as to whether he would have done better to take the more experienced of the two available men. We cannot help thinking of Whymper, and of how, on that great day when he launched his attack on the Matterhorn, he included a beginner among his team.[1]

When Mallory reached the North Col his companions noted that his usual good humour seemed to have deserted him. Was the responsibility for the climb weighing heavily upon him, or was he ' under the weather ' as a result of the laryngitis which was giving him trouble ?

He had decided not to take the usual route up the North Face itself, but to make straight for the East Ridge and follow it to the

[1] The first ascent of the Matterhorn, in July 1865, cost the lives of four men. On the way down Hadow slipped, carrying away the guide, Michel Croz, Hudson, and Lord Francis Douglas. Only Whymper and the two Taugwalder guides escaped with their lives, the rope breaking between them and their unfortunate companions.

summit. The Ridge would certainly be more exposed to the wind, but the ground itself would no doubt be easier to negotiate, being devoid of the smooth and sloping slabs which had proved too dangerous an obstacle in every previous attempt. The ridge was broken, however, by two great ' steps ' (see map, p. 75), and it remained to be seen whether it was possible to get either over them or round them. It was impossible, from a distance and through binoculars, to make out how difficult these obstacles might prove. In any case, one never can tell from a distance whether any particular ' pitch,' or section of a climb, is possible or not. One can be certain only at close range, and it is often only then that the vital handhold or cleft in the rock suddenly strikes the eye.

Mallory took with him only a small number of oxygen cylinders, as he did not intend using them until beyond Camp 6, but despite the fact that the appliances had been modified and lightened since 1922 they were still very heavy, forming, together with clothing and a day's rations, a total individual load of about thirty-six pounds.

On June 6 Mallory and Irvine started out for Camp 5 with a small group of Sherpas. On the following day, as they went on up to Camp 6, Odell in his turn reached Camp 5, thus providing the support which had now come to be recognized as a necessary part of the Everest technique. Soon after his arrival Odell heard the porters returning from Camp 6, to a dangerous accompaniment of loosened stones. They brought word from Mallory that the weather was perfect, but that the oxygen appliances were " devilishly awkward " on the move.

That evening, after the porters had gone, Odell was left alone at Camp 5, over 24,200 feet up, and from the tiny ledge of rocks where his tent was pitched he gazed at the vista before him. It presented a striking spectacle of majestic grandeur. The enormous pyramid of Everest, " the nearest thing to God on earth," blocked out part of the skyline, its dark mass throwing into contrast the pale opalescence of the far-off Tibetan plateaux. Around the Rongbuk Glacier the snowy peaks gradually turned yellow, pink, and purple, while mauve and blue-tinted abysses opened at their feet. A hundred miles away to the east the white mass of Kanchen-junga lay as though afloat, its outlines blurred and softened in mist. Odell had seen many remarkable sunsets, but this one seemed to surpass them all. It was a " sublime and ineffable crowning point " that was never to fade from his memory.

Alone at great heights, a man seems somehow raised to a higher pitch of awareness ; having no one to talk to, he listens to the voice of Nature. His relationship with her becomes more intimate ; he feels that at last he understands her, and it is as though he were

E

on the point of initiation into all her secrets. He identifies himself
with her ; he has become the fold in the snow, the patch of sky
between two clouds, he is part of the lofty peak, the blue abyss,
the rock glowing red in the sun, and his heart is full like the heart
of a lover. . . .

As Odell closed the flap of his tent and shut out the encouraging
vision of the sky he thought of his friends at Camp 6 ; they too
would be falling asleep, and their hopes would be high. Unless,
of course, Mallory was lying awake, unable to sleep at the thought
that the highest mountain in the world was " capable of severity,
a severity so awful and so fatal that the wiser sort of men do well
to think and tremble even on the threshold of their high endeavour."[1]

Next day Odell went up to Camp 6. The sky, quite clear early
in the morning, was already becoming overcast. Clouds were
coming in quickly from the west and scudding across the mountain ;
they gave no occasion for alarm, however, for they were not dense
or heavy. From the way they gleamed in the sun it seemed as
though the summit of Everest must be clear of cloud.

Odell made a detour across the North Face ; being a geologist,
he was interested in the structure of the mountain, which he thought
to consist of a bed-rock of gneiss overlaid with limestone and broken
by seams of light-coloured granitoid rock.

Just as he reached the top of a steep slope the clouds parted
above him, and both ridge and summit, powdery with snow against
the blue sky, suddenly came into view. Then, as he watched, he
saw in the far distance a small, moving black dot standing out on
a snow-covered slope leading to one of the Steps. It was followed
by a second dot. The first moved upward at a good pace to the
top of the Step. At that moment the clouds closed in again, and
Odell saw nothing more. He was quite sure that he had sighted
Mallory and Irvine, but was astonished that at ten minutes to one
they should still be at a point which according to Mallory's time-
table they should have reached by eight o'clock that morning.
What could have caused the delay ? Was it due to soft snow, or to
trouble with the oxygen equipment ?

On reaching Camp 6 Odell found things in some disorder.
Articles of clothing had been thrown down in the tent, together
with scraps of food and magnesium pellets, while pieces of metal
and duraluminium supports were lying all over the place. This
seemed to show that repairs to the oxygen equipment had become
necessary just as the two men were starting out.

It began to snow, and Odell took refuge in the tent. After a
time, however, it occurred to him that the bad weather would

[1] Howard-Bury, *Mount Everest : The Reconnaissance, 1921*, p. 279.

perhaps force the climbers to come down again, and in the event of that happening they might have difficulty in finding the camp. He therefore went out and started climbing up to meet them, stopping from time to time to whistle and yodel in case they might be within shouting distance, but the wind kept carrying the sound of his voice away in a flurry of snow. After an hour of this he went back down. When he reached Camp 6 the squalls, which had lasted no more than two hours, dropped to reveal once more the white, sunlit North Face. Odell carefully scrutinized the mountain; he was eager to catch a glimpse

A.J.V.

of his friends, but unfortunately the chances were poor. They would have to appear on the skyline of the ridge or stand out clearly on a patch of snow just as he looked in their direction.

It was getting late, and he decided to leave the camp, remembering that Mallory had advised him, in the message sent down with the porters, to evacuate Camp 6 and even Camp 5 before nightfall. This was necessary, as in each case the tent was intended to hold two men ; if Odell were to remain there when Mallory and Irvine returned one of them would have to sleep outside. This was out of the question at such a height, so, after eating some food, Odell left provisions in an obvious place, fastened the tent-doors, and left the camp. It was then 4.30 P.M.

On the way down he stopped from time to time and examined the slopes of the mountain in the hope of seeing something moving. It was getting late, and by now the two climbers should have been on their way back. He began to feel real anxiety.

Towards 6 P.M. he reached Camp 5 but did not stop. He was in such good form that he was able to make long ' glissades,' or sliding movements, standing upright on the snow. This saved a considerable amount of time, and in one hour he covered a distance normally requiring four.

At the North Col he found Hazard, who gave him tea and hot soup, and then for a long time the two men anxiously watched the mountain for a sign of their returning comrades. No light appeared, although Mallory had a lantern and even magnesium cartridges for use as distress signals. The evening sky was clear, and once the after-glow of sunset had died away the moon shed its soft light over the neighbouring mountains. There was a chance that its faint beams, reflected from the snow, might help the belated climbers on their way. . . .

Next morning Odell and Hazard resumed their watch, training their binoculars on the high-altitude camps, but there was no movement in the neighbourhood of the little tents. At noon, unable to stand the suspense, Odell decided to go back up and search for the missing men. Before he left he and Hazard agreed on a system of signals which would allow both day and night communication between the two camps. By day he was to lay sleeping-bags out on the snow ; by night he would signal with lights.

He then set off with two porters. Anxiety seemed to have given him the strength of ten, and he felt no fatigue, although only the day before he had made a considerable effort in climbing to a height of 26,000 feet.

On arriving at Camp 5 he was not surprised to find it deserted ;

he had not, in fact, expected to find his friends there, for if they had been he would have seen them moving about. The wind was sweeping across the North Ridge in violent squalls. Odell and the porters shivered throughout the night ; it was appallingly cold in the tents, and they were unable to sleep. As a result the porters next morning declared themselves incapable of going any farther, and Odell sent them down again ; he would go on alone, in spite of the wind, which was still as fierce as ever. He carried an oxygen cylinder, with the idea of reviving his flagging energies from time to time. The oxygen, in fact, did not help at all, Odell being no doubt sufficiently acclimatized by now to do without it.

Camp 6 turned out to be just as he had left it, except that one of the masts of the tent had broken in the wind ; the guy-ropes, however, had held. He jettisoned his oxygen equipment, and immediately went on again.

He continued climbing for nearly two hours, searching in vain for his two friends. What hope had he of finding them cn that gigantic mountain-side, that bleak and empty waste, storm-ravaged and utterly desolate ?

At last he gave up, and with heavy heart returned to his tent to shelter for a while. Taking advantage of an apparent lull, he dragged two sleeping-bags on to a steep, snow-covered slope and laid them out in the form of a letter ' T.' Hazard, on the North Col, would know from this signal that he had found no trace of the missing men. It was no easy matter to cut steps in the snow and pin the sleeping-bags down with stones ; the wind kept snatching them away, as if to prevent the news from becoming known.

As he was on the point of going down, Odell fastened the tent-door and looked back for the last time at the mighty peak as it emerged periodically from its covering of clouds. If only he could wrest from it the secret of their fate ! But the wind rose and fell, and in his ears it sounded like the voice of the pitiless mountain itself, raised in a scream of derisive laughter.

But then, as he watched it, his heart heavy within him, the face of the mountain seemed slowly to change. A suggestion of something else appeared in its wild and forbidding countenance, something strangely compelling, a sort of fascination. They too, poor devils, had felt its alluring charm, they had fallen victims to that magic spell and had climbed hopefully upward, oblivious of the journey home. . . .

Did They reach the Summit ?

The question arose as soon as the rest of the party were together again. Norton, fearing that the monsoon would break at any moment and take still more of his men, would not rest until they were all down at the Base Camp. One after the other the various camps were evacuated.

The members of the expedition were now doing their best to accept the loss of their comrades as sensibly as possible, as they had been taught to do by the 1914 War. But at every moment something would remind them of the missing men—an empty tent, two vacant places at table. . . . A great sadness weighed down upon them. They decided to raise a memorial in honour of the twelve men, some British, some Himalayan, who had lost their lives during the various attempts on the mountain. On the moraine above the Base Camp they built a great pyramid of stones, over twelve feet high, and on it they set plaques bearing the names of the three Britons—Kellas, Mallory, and Irvine—together with those of the nine native porters who had likewise perished.

As soon as they were gathered together the talk turned to what had now become an obsession with them : had Mallory and Irvine been the victims of an accident ? Had they bivouacked somewhere and frozen to death ? Had they reached the summit of Everest before they were lost ?

Every one thought it impossible that Mallory could have been guilty of carelessness ; he was too good a climber for that, too steeped in the Alpine Club's traditions of mountaineering wisdom to have taken any foolish chances. So what could have led him to his destruction ?

Everest alone knew the answer, and the Great Peak told no tales. That year the mountain had made cruel war on the human invader. It had taken two lives at the outset, then it had waited ; allowing its opponents to come within striking distance, it had deliberately chosen its victims, and then, in one fell swoop, it had savagely wiped out two of the bravest and the best.

A.J.Y.

CHAPTER VII

THE FLIGHT OVER EVEREST

IN the opinion of the Dalai Lama the tragic events of 1924 were a sign that the Gods of the Mountain were angry, and he now refused permission for further attempts on Everest.

Pending a fresh decision, the British turned their attention to the possibility of flying over the mountain; this would give an opportunity to examine and photograph the mysterious South Face and to draw up maps of its immediate surroundings.

The project at once raised a serious problem; no aeroplane was then capable of flying high enough to cross Everest. It was calculated that a machine able to reach at least 33,000 feet would be needed, since it was indispensable to have a safety margin over and above 29,000 feet sufficient to offset the atmospheric irregularities and treacherous down-currents.

Research was carried out with these requirements in mind, and a Westland biplane was fitted with an extra-powerful engine and a modified fuselage.

The pilot was to sit in an open cockpit, protected from the wind by a Triplex screen, while the observer was to occupy a small closed cabin with sliding roof and side-screens. Pilot and observer were to be linked by telephone, and both would wear oxygen masks and electrically heated under-garments.

The photographic cameras were to be similarly heated as a protection against the frost which would otherwise put them out of action.

As soon as the aeroplane was ready tests were carried out in England. These were not always successful ; during the first flight, for example, the pilot began to lose consciousness as a result of the feed-pipe having broken away from his oxygen mask. The observer was preparing to bale out when fortunately the pilot succeeded in connecting up his mask and righting the machine.

Meanwhile permission to fly over Nepal had been applied for, and in 1933 the request was granted. It was now the devout hope of the organizers that the flight would pass off without incident.

In the event of an accident a rescue expedition would have to set out—on foot—and diplomatic complications would immediately arise, as the Government of Nepal had always been hostile to any attempt to enter its territory.

Two aeroplanes were to carry out the flight from the aerodrome at Purnea, on the Indian plain a few miles from the frontier of Nepal ; and they were expected to reach Everest in two hours.

Every day the impatient airmen telephoned Darjeeling for information as to weather conditions. It was important that the north-west wind, which is constant during the period immediately preceding the monsoon, should not be too strong, otherwise the aeroplanes flying into it would be slowed down, and might run out of fuel on the return trip.

Finally, on April 3 conditions seemed favourable, and the two machines took off, rising through the dense haze set up by the heat and dust of the Indian plain. Soon the tiny white triangle of Everest, flanked to the east by its ' twin,' Makalu, was sighted at a distance of eighty miles, the two peaks appearing to float above the mist like the unreal forerunners of some fantastic dream. . . .

Distances change rapidly, however, in the air. Everest grew larger, came steadily nearer, like a picture on a cinema screen, while beneath the wings of the planes there rose and fell a white surge of snow-covered peaks cleft by dark precipices. To the right rose the glittering, fearsome massif of Kanchenjunga.

As they flew onward the airmen caught sight of the ' white plume ' of Everest, streaming out for about six miles in the direction of Makalu. The members of preceding expeditions had always been puzzled by the cloud which Everest wears like a feather in its hat, even in fine weather ; perhaps the airmen would be able to explain it ?

They were now quite near the mountain. Just as they were about to fly over Lhotse, separated only by the hollow of the South Col from Everest (see map, p. 41), they were caught in a down-current, and dropped nearly 1700 feet. Would they manage to get over the obstacle ?

Luckily, they were now gaining height, for the summit of Everest was hurtling towards them, and they were flying so close to the ground that for a moment they feared that the tails of the respective aircraft might hit something. By now, however, they were over the sheer walls of the North Face.

They turned, flew back, and for a quarter of an hour circled happily like fantastic birds over the highest mountain in the world. Each time that they tried to enter the ' plume ' itself they flew straight into furious gusts of wind and particles of ice which were flung against the fuselage with such force that one of the windows was broken.

The airmen had never flown through a cloud like this. In fact, it was not a cloud at all, but a sort of maelstrom set up by the north-west wind which ' lifts ' over the topmost ridge and sweeps down the South Face, carrying fragments of snow and ice in its swirling eddies. The latter then immediately resume their circular movement, but are gradually overcome, carried onward, and drawn out laterally over considerable distances by the main current of the wind.

The many photographic records brought back from this and from a second airborne expedition carried out a fortnight later afforded no important information regarding the structure either of the southern slope or of the final ridge. This was because a ridge seen from an aircraft—*i.e.*, from directly overhead—always seems to change its shape ; either it looks flatter than it really is or else its height is exaggerated. In order to have an idea of its relief and gradient the airmen would have had to fly for some time alongside the ridge, or, better still, below it. In view of the wind

E*

The Aircraft approaching Everest ; on the right, Makalu

A.J.VEILHAN

and atmospheric conditions this would have certainly meant disaster.

In the circumstances, however, the flight over Everest was a remarkable performance for the time at which it was accomplished, and one of which British aviation has every right to be proud.

A.J.V.

CHAPTER VIII

THE 1933 EXPEDITION

Labour in Vain

THE Dalai Lama finally gave way and, by authorizing a new expedition, brought to an end the quiet and peaceful period of truce which Everest had enjoyed since 1924. In 1933 the Great Peak was once again to see climbing towards it another long procession of human insects ; once more a few of the insects would detach themselves from the rest and threaten the summit itself.

Nine years had passed since the preceding expedition, and new men were needed to form a team. Under the leadership of Ruttledge thirteen climbers were collected together. Among those chosen, Smythe, Shipton, Greene, Birnie, Wood Johnson, Boustead, Crawford, and Shebbeare already had considerable Himalayan experience, especially Smythe and Shipton, who had taken part in the 1931 expedition to Kamet. The others—Wyn Harris, Wager, Longland, Brocklebank, and MacLean—although newcomers to the Himalayas, were all good climbers, and, with the exception of Shebbeare, whose age handicapped him, were all capable of taking part if necessary in the final assault.

At the time of the flights over Everest the expedition was just reaching the end of its approach march through Sikkim and Tibet. Base Camp was set up on the Rongbuk Glacier, followed by Camps 1, 2, and 3 on the orthodox sites.

By May 8 the climbing teams were ready to start. Once more the first step was to open up the route to the North Col, and this year the task took no fewer than four days to complete. Every morning, after a few hours of sunshine, work was interrupted by stormy weather. As soon as the men went down to shelter in their tents down came the snow, filling up the steps which they had just cut, and next day they would have to be cleared all over again. True, a good kick was usually enough, but the extra work hampered the daily schedule.

Like Mallory in 1924, Smythe ran into a serious obstacle when half-way up—a slightly overhanging wall of ice twenty feet high. Fortunately, he too was a sound performer on glaciers. He cut steps and handholds, drove in pitons (*i.e.*, iron spikes) and got Shipton to support him with the head of an ice-axe, but when he tried to step on to the piton which he had just rammed home his foot slipped, and he narrowly escaped falling backward. He was able to use his ice-axe with one hand only, and had to hang on with the other to tiny, slippery holds, but finally succeeded in reaching the top by hauling himself up with the help of a special ice-piton driven into the ice. It was the most exhausting gymnastic feat he had ever attempted, and he ended up breathless but happy. A piece of real mountaineering, and a rich reward for the long uphill struggle that until now had been little better than a dreary chore.

As soon as Camp 4 was set up the weather took a definite turn for the worse, and for a week climbers and porters were cut off on the North Col, unable to show their faces outside their tents.

The camp stood in extraordinary surroundings. It had been pitched below the actual ridge of the Col, on the lower lip of a crevasse whose upper edge rose above the camp to a height of forty feet. The four tents were strung out along what looked like a rounded platform measuring about a hundred feet by sixteen.

The new Arctic tents were very big, and their octagonal shape gave them the appearance of Christmas puddings without their sprigs of holly. Camp 4 was no place for sleep-walkers. Two steps to the right on leaving the tents and one fell into the crevasse, two to the left and away one went down the steep, snow-covered slopes on to the Rongbuk Glacier.

The advantage of the site was that the camp was protected from wind ; the disadvantage was that it was exposed to avalanches falling from the upper slopes. Usually they fell into the crevasse with the noise of an exploding bomb, spattering the tents with snow, and blowing a cloud of white powder through the flaps. But it only required a heavier mass of snow than usual to slip for the whole camp to be engulfed ; a catastrophe of this kind was to occur on Nanga Parbat in 1937, causing sixteen deaths. Some time later a heavy fall of snow caused sufficient anxiety for the camp to be moved to the Col itself. The wind was preferable, after all, to burial alive.

That year Camp 4 was equipped with a telephone, a ground line having been run with great difficulty up the mountain-side, but unfortunately the cable was not quite long enough. The end was therefore left sticking up on a ridge of snow while the box with its battery was stowed in a tent. Every time one of the party wished to use the telephone he had to tuck the box under his arm, climb on to the crest of snow, and sit astride it while he connected the wires with half-frozen fingers. He was then free to try to make himself heard above the clamour of the wind.

Messages were telephoned in this way to Camp 3 and passed on from there to the Base Camp, which retransmitted them in its turn by radio to Darjeeling. Thus in a succession of relays the *Daily Telegraph* received messages from the North Col in a matter of hours.

News bulletins were sent up in the opposite direction, and by this means the climbers heard, one fine day, that they would have to press on with the assault, as the monsoon had made its appearance in the Bay of Bengal.

The plan of attack had been discussed at great length by the members of the expedition during the sea-crossing, the approach march, and the setting up of the various camps. They were naturally quite certain that " this time " they would reach the summit. The question was whether, after the first team had succeeded, the second would be allowed to climb to the top in its turn. Chickens will, no doubt, always be counted before they are hatched !

It was no easy matter to organize the comings and goings of

the various climbing-parties in order to have a suitable team in the right place and at the right time for the final assault when ' D-Day ' came, and it was even more difficult to work out the number of porters necessary for the setting up of the various camps. It was always advisable to hold a number of extra men in reserve, since allowance had to be made for sickness and fatigue, not to mention the whims of the weather, which could always upset the movement plan, however good the organization might be.   Finally, it was always a good thing to have a white man with a knowledge of Nepalese at the high-altitude camps to keep up the Sherpas' morale in case of need.

The question is often asked as to why a soldier—usually a colonel or a general—has so often been chosen to lead the various Everest expeditions.   The answer is simple : the work of the expedition leader is similar in many respects to that of a senior staff-officer in the field.

In the light of previous experience, the principle was accepted in 1933 that it was impossible to cover in one single stage the two thousand yards of broken ground separating Camp 6 from the summit.   Should plans be made, therefore, for setting up a seventh camp ?   Or would it be better to gain height by establishing Camps 5 and 6 at points higher up than before ?

Discussions sometimes became heated, every one airing his own pet theory " with a regrettable contempt for the feelings of his contradictors," as Shipton put it.   One of the odd consequences of oxygen-shortage is its irritating effect on the human character. Climbers would get into such a state that they could no longer stand the sight of one another.   The way in which a man ate, drank, smoked, or slept—even the patch on his trousers—anything, in fact, would become exasperating.

However, after receiving the monsoon bulletin from Darjeeling, the group of climbers on the North Col were all agreed that the assault must be made without delay.   The weather was fine, but dark and ominous clouds could already be seen to the south.   How long would the Tibetan wind keep at a respectful distance ?

One team started off and set up Camp 5, five hundred feet higher than in 1924 ; then a second team, including Smythe and Shipton, moved off the following day.

Shipton felt like an athlete the night before a race.   He could hardly believe that the long-awaited moment had come at last, yet his keenness was mixed with anxiety : what sort of ' show ' would he put up at 28,000 feet ?   Would he still be in a fit state to climb ?

His worries were quite unnecessary, for as soon as he reached

Camp 5 the weather broke and all the climbing-parties were held up.

There was nothing for it but to wait, lying stretched out in one's sleeping-bag. " I doubt if anyone could claim to enjoy life at high altitudes," wrote Eric Shipton, with his usual engaging frankness, " enjoy, that is, in the ordinary sense of the word . . . smoking is impossible ; eating tends to make one vomit ; the necessity of reducing weight to a bare minimum forbids the importation of literature beyond that supplied by the labels on tins of food. . . ." [1]

At lower altitudes reading was the major stand-by of climbers living under canvas ; it helped them to kill time. All agreed that the most precious part of the expedition's equipment, and the thing that was handled with greatest care on the move, was the case of books.

For Shipton the hours seemed to drag by endlessly as he sat there learning those multicoloured labels by heart. " There is nothing to look at but the bleak confusion inside the tent and the scaly, bearded countenance of one's companion—fortunately the noise of the wind usually drowns the sound of his stuffy breathing —I used to try to console myself with the thought that a year ago I would have been thrilled by the very idea of taking part in our present adventure, a prospect that had then seemed like an impossible dream ; but altitude has the same effect upon the mind as upon the body, one's intellect becomes dull and unresponsive, and my only desire was to finish the wretched job and to get down to a more reasonable clime. . . ." [2]

During the night " the storm reached moments of unbelievable ferocity," wrote Smythe in his turn,

and although our tents were securely pegged and weighted with boulders it seemed possible that at any moment they would be blown away and we with them. The climax came when one of the side pegs was torn from its fastenings. Shipton and I were lying side by side in our sleeping-bags when this occurred. Instantly the tent billowed in like a well-filled sail. Something had to be done and done at once. Shipton did his best to support the fabric whilst I bundled on my wind-proof jacket and boots, then crawled outside into a maelstrom of whirling snow. So frightful was the hurricane that it was impossible to stand upright and I had to crawl on hands and knees in search of the lost guy-rope. It was not yet quite dark and I remember seeing a faint streak of green sky through a whirling rush of wind-borne snow. I remember, too, groping about in the smother until, more by luck than anything, my

[1] Eric Shipton, *Upon that Mountain* (Hodder and Stoughton, 1943), p. 119.
[2] *Ibid.*, p. 120.

A.J.V.

gloved hand lit on the loose rope. Then came the task of pulling the tent as taut as possible and attaching the rope to a boulder. This took a long time, and when at last it was done I was so exhausted that I barely had the strength to crawl into the tent, where I collapsed on my sleeping-bag, scarcely able to breathe.[1]

Smythe had to be massaged for hours before the circulation began to return to normal in his ice-cold limbs.

As soon as there was a lull in the storm the whole party went down, having finally abandoned the plan to set up Camp 6. The porters were suffering from frost-bite, and as a result two of them lost fingers.

They Try Again

When the weather improved Camp 5 was reoccupied and Camp 6 set up at 27,550 feet—650 feet higher than in 1924.

Unfortunately, the porters, who had kept going splendidly, were caught by the storm on the way down. It broke over them without warning just as they were getting back on to the North Ridge. There had been for some time an understanding that porters returning from the higher camps should for safety's sake be accompanied by a white man. Longland, who was in the lead, had great difficulty in finding his way back. The landscape was blotted out behind curtains of snow that billowed and swirled in the shrieking blast. Goggles were coated with ice, and had to be removed. Then their eyelashes froze and stuck together so that they could no longer see. Yet on they went, leaning sideways against the hurricane and packed close up to one another as they moved forward. Longland kept counting them to make sure that none were lost on the way, and at last brought his party safely back to the North Col.

The following day they were able to form some idea of what they had been through on discovering that one of their number was half-crazed. Poor old Kipa flatly refused to budge from his tent, believing himself to be dead. And since no corpse has ever been known to walk, there could be no question of his bestirring himself and making his way down to Camp 3. He was quite adamant, and had to be dragged down the slopes with Greene applying from behind, in order to shift him, what he termed " therapeutic propulsion." At the rope-ladder stage he was handed down from one to another like a parcel. Ruttledge came to meet the party, and, grabbing him round the waist, engaged him in a discussion (for Kipa was voluble in death) on where precisely lay

[1] Frank Smythe, *The Adventures of a Mountaineer* (Dent, 1940), pp. 195–196.

the boundary between the quick and the dead ! It was some weeks before Kipa recovered his mental balance, and even then he remained convinced that he had died and had been brought back to life by the doctor's magic powers. As we shall see, this kind of mental derangement was not to be confined to the porters.

It had been agreed that the party making the first assault should reconnoitre the route so strongly recommended by Mallory —the way along the great East Ridge.

On May 29 the teams were in position and duly spaced out : Wyn Harris and Wager at Camp 6, Smythe and Shipton at Camp 5, with a few climbers back in support at the North Col camp.

Up at Camp 6 Wyn Harris and Wager had a bad night with very little sleep. The platform on which their tent was pitched sloped outward, and was so tiny that the ground-sheet overshot it and hollowed out into a pocket overhanging space. Consequently the occupants had to be constantly shoving each other away with knees and elbows to avoid overlaying and suffocating each other.

At six in the morning the two men set off, the weather being fine. For an hour they climbed in the shadow and suffered a good deal from the cold. So with the first rays of sunlight they halted, took off their boots, and gave their feet a hard rub.

They made their way up diagonally towards the ridge. Some sixty feet short of it Wyn Harris, who was in the lead, found an ice-axe on a flat slab of rock. It appeared quite new, and the shining metal bore the name of a maker in the Zermatt valley. The two climbers were quite sure that here was the axe of either Mallory or Irvine. However, they left it for the time being where it lay and pushed forward.

They approached the First Step, which is in the form of two great towers (see map, p. 99). Initially they had intended to work round it, returning to the ridge on the far side. But, seen from close quarters, that part of the ridge looked very uneven, and following it would clearly be a long job.

In the Alps, ridges are greatly in favour as ways up a mountain, because on them there is no danger from falling stones and avalanches. In the Himalayas, on the other hand, it is now realized that they are better avoided, on account of the deep indentations they present and the quantities of snow and ice which collect upon them.

Wyn Harris and Wager were only too well aware of this, and considered it wiser to move on at a lower level to where the Second Step rises up. They were working on easy terrain, and considered it unnecessary to rope themselves together.

On reaching the foot of the Second Step they saw that it was impossible to climb straight over it. It was a formidable obstacle, cleaving the air like the prow of a battleship, and eighty feet high ! Like the First Step, it had to be by-passed. The climbers then noticed a vertical gully to the rear of the Step and running up to the Ridge. If they could manage to climb up it there would be nothing to prevent them from going on to the summit !

They reached the foot of the gully, and after one look roped themselves together. The walls overhung horribly in many places ; in addition the rock was smooth, and the only footholds available were a number of nondescript bumps for the most part covered with snow. As for handholds, there were none. Wyn Harris began climbing, but did not even run out the full length of the rope. At sea-level he would probably have made light of the climb, difficult though it was, but here at 28,000 feet his strength was inadequate, and he gave up. It certainly looked as if Norton was right, and the route following the ridge impossible.

The two men now had to retrace their steps, having completed their mission, but they then realized that it was still early and that they were not far from the Great Couloir. They therefore decided to carry out a reconnaissance in that direction.

They crossed over to the right, following ledges which brought them to the edge of the Couloir, but had considerable difficulty in getting into the gully itself owing to the fact that the steep and snow-covered slabs sloped in the wrong direction. There is nothing more treacherous than thick snow on slabs of rock ; sometimes the whole mass will slide off *en bloc*. The two men moved forward extremely slowly. They were unable to belay each other, as there was nothing to pass the rope around—not even the tiniest projection on the rock.

Finally they reached the bed of snow in the lowest part of the Couloir ; this turned out to be soft and powdery, and slid away as soon as it was touched. Placing their feet as carefully as possible, they nevertheless went on, and carried out a sensational traversing movement—sensational in view of the fact that the Couloir drops 10,000 feet into the depths of the Rongbuk Glacier.

The wall of rock enclosing the Couloir on the opposite side was more thickly covered with snow than the side which they had just left. The upper slopes of the North Face are in some ways similar to those of the north face of the Eiger, in that the rocks slope downward into empty space with not even a suspicion of a ledge or other irregularity to encourage the climber and delight his weary eye. Footholds and handholds are littered with loose stones that ask nothing better than to roll away downward under their treacherous covering of snow. Some mountains can be said

F

to ' play the game ' where the climber is concerned, but others—
and Everest is one of them—seem determined from the start to
hurl him to his doom.

Nevertheless Wyn Harris and Wager carefully and slowly began
to climb, and reached a small secondary gully full of loose snow.
Wyn Harris tried to get across, but the snow gave way under his
foot and cascaded downward. It would never take his full weight.
Wager was standing on a slab, doing his best to keep his balance,
and quite unable to belay his partner. Wyn Harris saw that he
had gone as far as he could without risking disaster, and came
down again.

The two men then held a council of war. The climb did not
seem absolutely impossible, yet in present conditions it was certainly
very dangerous. . . . They estimated that they had reached the
point attained by Norton in 1924, and that they were therefore
a thousand feet from the summit. Even if all went well they could
not climb a thousand feet in less than four hours. It was now
already half-past twelve, and they must be back at Camp 5 before
nightfall, since Smythe and Shipton would be at Camp 6 that
evening.

Well, there was no point in tempting the devils of the mountain,
and they turned back. British climbers deserve full credit for the
common sense they have always shown in giving up at the right
time. It is always a difficult decision to make, and with so much
at stake there is always a strong temptation to press on ' by guess
and by God.'

The two men were so disappointed at the idea of returning
empty-handed that they decided at least to climb on to some part
of the Ridge—anywhere would do—to see what possibilities it
offered. Wager, in a supreme single-handed effort, reached the
crest, to the east of the First Step, and became the first climber
to see the South Face of Everest ! It was the Ridge, however,
which held his attention. It turned out to be sharp-edged, indented,
and quite apart from the two Steps, defended by ' gendarmes ! ' [1]
An ascent via the Ridge would clearly be out of the question.
Wager then rejoined Wyn Harris and the two men slowly made
their way down to Camp 6.

There they found Smythe and Shipton, who had just arrived.
They advised them to waste no time on the Ridge, but to follow
from the outset the transversal route taken by Norton ; they then
went down, taking the missing men's ice-axe with them.

There was to be much argument regarding that axe, which
had lain there, waiting, for nine years, and it was to shed an un-

[1] Pinnacles of rock standing on a ridge.

certain light on the tragic events in which it had undoubtedly played a part.

It could not have been deliberately thrown away. A mountaineer and his ice-axe are inseparable ; the axe is his best friend, and his greatest safeguard. It could not have fallen from above ; owing to the slope of the rocks it would never have stopped once it began to slide. When Somervell, in 1922, inadvertently dropped his ice-axe, it swiftly bounced out of sight into the chasms of the Rongbuk Glacier. This axe, therefore, must have been put where it was

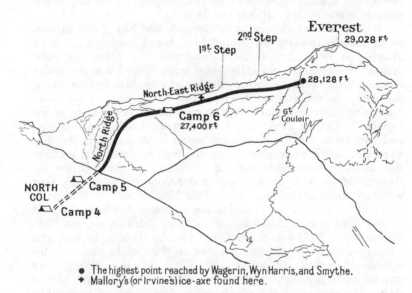

● The highest point reached by Wager in, Wyn Harris, and Smythe.
+ Mallory's (or Irvine's) ice-axe found here.

found. And quite understandably the imagination conjured up a picture of one of the climbers slipping and his partner hastily putting down his ice-axe to grab the rope with both hands. . . . All the evidence indicated that it marked the scene of the accident.

It was assumed that Mallory and Irvine had been roped together, and this was probably the case. The climbers might well have dispensed with the rope on the easier rocks of the North Face, but Mallory had possibly considered that it was an indispensable precaution on the Ridge. And so the rope linking the men together had probably caused the death of them both.

However, even without the rope there was another possible explanation of the double fall. One of the climbers might have fallen on top of the other when they happened to be close together.

There is always a tendency to overlook a perfectly feasible combination of adverse factors, and yet such a combination is more
often than not the cause of such disasters.

Had the accident occurred on the upward or the downward
climb ? If Odell was right in claiming to have seen them moving
up the Ridge, and at a greater height than that at which the axe
was found, the accident could only have taken place on the way
back—*i.e.*, while the pair were climbing downward. But had
Odell really seen them ? Doubts arose when the story was told of
the optical illusion experienced by Eric Shipton on the day of the
attempt made by Wyn Harris and Wager.

Shipton was on his way up to Camp 6, and had almost arrived
when Smythe, moving up behind him, heard him shout, " Wyn
Harris and Wager are at the Second Step ! " There was good
reason for excitement, for if the other team crossed that particular
obstacle there would be nothing further to stop them from reaching
the top. The two men sat down to get a better view. They could
quite clearly see two black dots on the snow-covered slope at the
foot of the Second Step. They watched the black dots carefully,
and saw them move. A moment or so later, however, the dots
were still in the same place. Smythe and Shipton then realized
that the dots were rocks sticking up out of the ice. Higher up
they could see two more, above the Second Step, and as they
watched them *they* moved too. This kind of optical illusion is
frequent in the mountains, and many a climber has been deceived
in the same way. Could it not be that Odell's eyes, too, had
deceived him ? It was remembered that he thought he had seen
Mallory and Irvine through a break in the clouds, and only for
a moment or two. It had seemed to him that the climbers were
moving up at a good pace ; the fact was that the difficulty of that
particular section of the climb made fast climbing impossible.
Odell said later that he was not sure whether he had seen the First
or the Second Step. If it was the First, then Mallory and Irvine
were incredibly late at the time, since at 1 P.M. they were only
reaching the point where Wyn Harris and Wager had arrived at
7 A.M., the latter party having started, admittedly, from a slightly
greater height.

Most people tended to favour the theory that the accident had
happened on the way down, because on sloping ground climbers
are more likely to fall in the direction in which they are moving.
Were the two men on their way back from the summit ? Had
they succeeded ? Few think so to-day. Hillary, having seen the
East Ridge and the North Face from the top of Everest, has
declared that they both looked to him absolutely unclimbable.

Another Failure

" There is not much *joie de vivre* in high-altitude mountaineering ; it is a dull, plodding business, inexpressibly tedious and enervating," remarks Smythe.

At Camp 6, after Wyn Harris and Wager had gone, Shipton and Smythe were preparing their supper. Himalayan mountaineers have always complained of the trouble involved in cooking a meal in high-altitude camps. Smythe and Shipton, for example, found themselves panting for breath from the mere act of slipping into the low tent ; they then had to battle with a cooker that either refused to work or else stank like the oil-stove used by Mallory—all in a confined space. Half reclining in their sleeping-bags, they had to watch every movement so as not to knock the shaky little contraption over. One careless movement and the supper would be done for and the tent on fire. The number of utensils at their disposal being strictly limited, they made tea in the saucepan used for cooking, with the result that the beverage produced was more like Tibetan tea than the English variety, with circles of grease in it, and particles of food left over from every course—sometimes from the meals of the previous day.

That evening at Camp 6 the two climbers used the solid-fuel or ' Tommy ' cooker familiar to British soldiers, as their Primus refused to work at high altitudes. With this tiny appliance it took them an hour to melt a saucepanful of snow. Hot drinks were all that they could swallow with comfort, their throats being painfully tender ; they were sick of the sweet and rather dainty foodstuffs with which they had been provided, and equally sick of the sweets which they had been sucking on the way up. Sweets being easier to eat than anything else, they generally preferred to go without other food during the climb on account of the cold and wind. That night they could have done with something more substantial. Shipton thought longingly of a dozen eggs, Smythe conjured up visions of sauerkraut and frankfurters.

While they were finishing supper the tent was suddenly lit up. They opened the flap and looked out at the sunset ; it was an exceptionally calm evening and only at rare intervals were the walls of the lonely little tent shaken by puffs of wind so icy cold that they might have come straight from the lungs of the legendary demon who rules the Tibetan Hell. Hundreds of feet below rolled a sea of golden clouds from which there emerged, like rocks from the ocean, a number of peaks that flamed and glowed in the rays of the setting sun. Very soon, however, the colours died away, and clouds and mountains took on a cold and grey appearance.

Shivering, the two men closed the tent door and got down into their sleeping-bags.

They spent a very bad night ; it was as if the sharpest stones in the whole of Asia had chosen to collect together under their ground-sheet, and their sleep was constantly broken as they tossed and turned and rolled on top of each other, half smothered in the process.

They awoke at dawn, tired and aching, to find that a blizzard was in progress, driving clouds of snow across the mountain. They would have to wait, so they fastened the door of the tent.

They spent the day in their sleeping-bags, discussing the dangers in which the storm might involve them. They wondered, too, whether the monsoon might not have broken, in which case their chances of getting back alive were slim indeed, since it would be impossible to withdraw to the North Col while the storm was at its height. True, they had enough food for three days, but only two days' fuel. Then what would happen ? At that height it is so cold that a human being can only survive with the help of hot drinks. . . . The most they could hope for was that the storm would blow over and allow them to continue climbing, but even then they would have difficulty with so much fresh snow on the ground. It was likely, too, that the hold-up would accelerate the process of physical deterioration, and this would finally undo the beneficial effects of acclimatization. Fortunately, the kind of lethargy into which they had sunk brought its own compensation in the form of an almost blissful indifference.

As the day drew to its close the wind died down and the clouds thinned out. Through the skylight of the tent they could see the summit of Everest. Shipton was surprised to see how close they were. " Well," he wrote later, " 1600 feet was not far ; without the powder snow on the rocks and in sea-level conditions we could climb it in an hour ! An ambition of a lifetime and we were too weak to grasp it ! " [1]

The next night was no better than the first, but on the following morning the sky was clear. The two men then slowly began to get ready. Their boots were like lumps of granite, and had to be thawed out for a long time over the flame of a candle. They put on garment after garment ; five pairs of socks, two pairs of long woollen under-pants, seven sweaters, and a wind-proof jacket with a hood covering a woollen Balaclava helmet. Shipton writes that he felt " about as suitably equipped for delicate rock climbing as a fully rigged deep-sea diver for dancing a tango." [2]   Yet despite

[1] *Upon that Mountain.*, p. 126.
[2] *Ibid.*, p. 126.

all those layers of clothing the cold went right through them as soon as they left the tent. It was then 7.30 A.M., and the wind had fallen.

By mutual agreement they did not rope themselves together. Very slowly they moved upward, pausing at frequent intervals. Eric Shipton felt unwell ; his stomach was giving him trouble, and he felt " as weak as a kitten." . . . " Anyone seeing us leave Camp 6," wrote Smythe, " would have said : ' There go two crocks who ought to be in hospital ! ' " [1]

Acting upon the advice given them by Wyn Harris and Wager, the two men immediately took the route followed by Norton, and climbed up the slabs of the Yellow Band. The wind had swept the snow away in some places, but had collected it together in others, hiding footholds and handholds and masking the loose stones on the sloping slabs. They took particular care as they moved into the area where they thought Mallory and Irvine had slipped and fallen to their death.

Two hours later Shipton became really ill, and said he could go no farther. The two friends had always agreed that if one of them grew tired he would stop before his strength gave out completely, so as not to make things difficult for his partner, and also so as to get down unaided.

Shipton's withdrawal was a severe blow for Smythe, but he had no intention of giving up. He had come to climb Everest, and climb it he would, alone if need be. At the time that seemed to him the natural thing to do, and he saw nothing particularly daring about it.

He first made sure that Shipton was in a fit state to get back to Camp 6, and then continued. From now on, like Norton, he would have to fight single-handed. But *was* he really alone ? Ever since he had left Shipton he had felt as though some one had come behind him and taken his companion's place, some one whose friendly and reassuring presence warded off all feeling of isolation. He constantly found himself looking behind, and was surprised each time to see that there was no one there ! . . .

Other mountaineers, climbing alone in the Alps, have experienced this kind of illusion. Jacques de Lépiney used to tell the story of how during one particular climb the idea of being alone had such an effect upon him that he fastened himself to a rope and let the end trail behind him so as to create the illusion of an imaginary companion. The illusion became so strong that after a time he could have sworn that there was some one on the end of his rope, and he too found it a very comforting feeling.

[1] *The Adventures of a Mountaineer*, p. 202.

When he found himself faced by the rocks of the buttress leading to the ' pyramid ' of the summit itself, for a moment Smythe's courage failed him.. They were steeper than anything he had met with so far, and above all they were covered with thick snow.

The four climbers who have so far reached this point—Norton, Wyn Harris, Wager, and Smythe have all declared since that the day those rocks were found to be clear of snow they would not prove very difficult to climb. Unfortunately, the rocks in question always *will* be covered with snow. The wind lifts it from the North Face and drives it into the Couloir as a broom sweeps dust into a crack in a floor, and once it has fallen on sheltered ground the wind can no more shift it than the broom can get into the crack in the floor and remove the dust.

Smythe realized then his chances of success were slim, but not for a moment did he think of giving in. He looked up. The summit, " an abrupt pyramid of yellow-coloured rock ending in a shining point of snow with the usual white plume streaming endlessly from it," seemed hundreds of miles away, and separated from him " by an impassable gulf of difficulty and fatigue." [1] And yet, hopeless as the struggle seemed, he went on climbing as high as he possibly could.

He then followed a ledge that led into the Couloir itself, but it grew gradually narrower, until nothing was left but handholds and footholds a few inches wide. At its narrowest point it led round the slight bulge of an otherwise vertical projection in the rock. Smythe moved cautiously on, reaching forward and feeling for slight irregularities in the surface, pinned to the wall with arms and legs stretched wide apart, and looking rather like the four-footed vermin ' crucified ' by farmers on the walls of their barns. He was just able to keep his balance, but the rock was forcing him backward. One deep breath and he would be over !

He worked his way back, and immediately felt that his courage had failed him. Surely it was only a matter of one step—one step, that needed a little self-confidence ! Just on the other side the ledge was wider. He tried once more . . . but his courage failed him again.

He then sought another solution. Twenty feet below he could see a good ledge leading to the great gully, and although unwilling to lose even a foot or two of the height that he had reached after such strenuous efforts, he decided to go down.

The ledge was broad, and after the recent strain upon his nerves he halted and relaxed for a few blissful moments. He then prepared to cross the snow in the Great Couloir, the bed of which sloped upward at an angle of 50 degrees. It was no longer the powdery

[1] *The Adventures of a Mountaineer*, pp. 203, 204.

snow found there two days before by Wyn Harris and Wager ; it was hard snow, probably as a result of avalanches which had rolled it flat, as is generally the case in gullies of this kind. Smythe then cut steps in the snow ; it was a terrible effort, and after every three or four strokes with the ice-axe he had to stop for breath, like a runner at the end of a quarter-mile race.

Twenty steps brought him to the buttress on the opposite side, where the steep, awkwardly sloping rock was covered with a layer of snow varying in thickness from two to two and a half feet. The snow, the worst kind possible, resembled castor-sugar, and when Smythe cleared it from the holds it streamed down with a hissing sound.

After an hour of exhausting work he found that he had only risen about fifty feet. A feeling of despair came over him. His limbs were trembling with fatigue, and his heart was beating as though it would burst. He looked up. The summit seemed far away, and he had the feeling that it was looking down in pitiless indifference at the poor wretch of a human being panting and struggling there in his efforts to get to the top.

Then he looked down, and saw hundreds of peaks lying as though flattened at his feet ; there, too, were the glaciers, and the dark Rongbuk Valley, and even the sun-gilded plateau of Tibet, where the clouds cast blue-tinted shadows. He had the feeling of being " engulfed in a profound and awful silence. I trod the very boundaries of life and death on the topmost pinnacle of the earth's surface." [1]

He glanced behind him, seeking the reassuring presence of that nameless companion of his—and was disappointed to find no one there. He was alone, very much alone. Fear suddenly gripped him, and his one thought was to get away, to escape from the terrifying walls that shut him in !

At that precise moment catastrophe nearly overtook him : the rock gave way beneath his foot. Luckily, he had driven his ice-axe into a crack in the rock, a procedure which he had adopted throughout the climb in the absence of proper footholds. He clung to the axe, and managed to check his fall in time, but it was a narrow escape. At the time, however, he was so overcome by fatigue that he did not realize how near he had been to disaster.

Contrary to what he had feared, the descent proved to be easier than the upward climb, and in a few minutes he was back in the bed of the Couloir. He then crossed to the other side and made his way back along the broken ledges of the Yellow Band.

It was then that he remembered that he had eaten nothing all

[1] *The Adventures of a Mountaineer*, p. 207.

F*

Looking East from Camp 5

day long. He stopped and took from his pocket the slice of mint-cake that he had taken with him as his sole supply of food. Carefully he divided it up, turned round, and offered part of it to his ' companion '—but once again there was no one there !

He had some difficulty in finding his way across the wilderness of slabs that lay between him and Camp 6. The rock demanded constant care : if it was yellow the nails on his boots would bite into it ; if it was whitish in colour it became slippery. For an exhausted man each change of surface was a potential danger.

He had nearly arrived when, looking up for once, he saw two strange black objects floating in the sky. The objects were shaped like ' blimps,' or observation balloons, but one had short, stubby wings, and the other a sort of protuberance shaped like the spout of a teapot. Both remained in the same position in the sky, but seemed to pulsate gently as though breathing. Smythe stopped, dumbfounded. He could make nothing of the apparition. Worried in case he might be going off his head, he proceeded to set himself one or two mental tests. He looked away, and immediately the objects disappeared from sight. He looked again at the place where they had been, and there they were again, just as before. He looked away a second time, and made an effort to focus his powers of concentration by identifying the peaks and glaciers of the surrounding country, but when he reverted to the black objects they were still there. Completely at a loss for an explanation, he was preparing to continue on his way when a cloud drew near and gradually hid everything. A few minutes later the cloud thinned out and the sky reappeared, empty ; the objects had gone.

The physical and nervous strain undergone by men climbing at very great heights could hardly find better demonstration than in tricks of the mind like these.

Two Difficult Descents

Smythe was so exhausted on reaching Camp 6 that he decided to spend a third night there, so in order to afford him a minimum of comfort, and also to reassure Birnie, who was in support at Camp 5, Shipton prepared to move down.

The weather had already deteriorated and clouds were beginning to envelop the mountain, but so far there was no sign of stormy conditions.

As a result of the snow which had fallen the night before, Shipton ran into trouble on the first section of the journey, for the rocks which he had negotiated with some difficulty on the way up turned out to be abominably dangerous during the downward climb. At one point he was clinging by his finger-tips, and was about to drop on to a patch of snow when suddenly the snow slid off, leaving a smooth slab of rock with nothing whatever to check his fall. He was left suspended with his feet dangling in space. Once he let go he would fall to his death. There was nothing for it but to get back up, and so, exerting every ounce of his strength in one horrible effort, he hauled himself up again.

When we realize that at 16,000 feet a man pants with the mere exertion of lighting his pipe, because his breath leaves him as he throws away the match, and his pipe goes out as he recovers his breath, we can appreciate the will-power that enabled Shipton, at 27,400 feet, to raise his body until his feet reached the level of his hands.

Shaken as he was by this narrow escape, he went straight on down ; he realized that a gale was approaching, and it was none too soon when he reached less difficult ground.

The gale burst upon him with such violence that he was unable to stay on his feet, and had to crouch against a rock with his back turned to the wind. Whenever the wind dropped he moved down in a series of rushes, but was blinded by clouds of driven snow and unable to see more than a few yards in front of him. He soon realized that he had lost all sense of direction and sat down helplessly to wait. . . .

" For those who wish to achieve complete philosophical detachment," he wrote later,

there is perhaps something to recommend life at high altitudes. The mind appears to be quite incapable of strong emotion of any sort. To be lost on a mountain-side in such circumstances would normally be an unpleasantly exciting experience to the calmest of men. I found it neither unpleasant nor exciting, and was blissfully resigned to whatever the fates chose to do with me.[1]

What the fates did, luckily for Shipton, was to cause the clouds to open and disclose a sharp-pointed peak which he was able to identify. Much as a navigator uses a lighthouse to get his bearings, he was able to steer by this peak, and found his way without further difficulty to Camp 5, where he spent the night.

Meanwhile Smythe, up at Camp 6, was listening to the moaning of the gale. According to whether the gusts of wind assailing the tent carried snow or not, the walls alternately rattled like a machine-gun and boomed like a drum. He thanked his stars that he had got back in time, but felt anxious regarding Shipton, struggling alone with the raging elements.

On Everest, however, squalls have the peculiar habit of coming

[1] *Upon that Mountain*, p. 128.

and going with the same almost unbelievable abruptness, and at sunset the wind fell. Before settling down for the night, Smythe unfastened the door of his tent and looked out.

" It was a scene of incredible desolation," he writes.

All round were great slabs of rocks mortared with snow in their interstices like an immense expanse of armour-plating. Thousands of feet beneath lay a great sea of cloud slowly writhing and twisting in its uppermost billows and, here and there, seeming almost on fire, where it was touched by the rays of the setting sun. There was no sound. No stone-fall or avalanche disturbed the serenity of Everest. There was silence, an absolute and complete silence ; and permeating all, investing all, with a deadly embrace, the coldness that reigns in the abysses of space.[1]

The calm was to be of short duration. During the night the wind raised its clamorous voice once more, but Smythe heard nothing. For thirteen hours on end he slept the deep sleep of exhaustion.

When he awoke next morning he was surprised to find himself half buried in snow. He soon realized what had happened ; he and Shipton had burned a small area of the tent fabric the night before with the flame of the cooker, and the wind had blown the snow in through the hole. Inside the tent it had formed a heap reaching half-way up to the roof, and covering everything—cooker, provisions, and the sleeper himself.

He had considerable difficulty in cooking his breakfast, since he had to grope in the snow for everything he needed, and it was so cold that he could not keep his hands out of the sleeping-bag for more than a few seconds at a time.

The air was calm on the way down, but he made slow progress, partly through weakness and partly because the rocks were covered with a thick coating of ice.

It was the first time that a climber had ever met glazed rocks on Everest at such a height, the sun being usually too weak to melt the snow, with the result that the rocks remain dry under their powdery covering. At 26,500 feet the only factors which can be relied upon to remove snow are evaporation—so intense on Everest that the snow is transformed from solid into vapour without passing through any transitional stage—and wind. The sun must have warmed the rocks to an exceptional degree for the first snow to have melted before it froze. This was a sign of the imminent arrival of the monsoon, with its warm winds, mild weather, and wet snow.

Smythe had not yet completed the hardest part of the descent

[1] *The Adventures of a Mountaineer*, p. 211.

when he noticed a strange, ragged-looking cloud scudding at staggering speed across the mountain-side. Before he could grasp what was happening he was struck by a squall of such incredible ferocity that he was nearly snatched from his hold on the rock. A second gust followed the first ; then came another, forcing him to drop to his knees and hang on. Several times he was lifted like a dead leaf, and it was only by driving the pick of his ice-axe deeply into the ground that he was able to break his fall. It was as though the great mountain were driving him away in a gust of hatred and rage, as if to get rid of him for once and for all.

Somehow Smythe managed to make his way to an easier part of the climb, but now, unfortunately, visibility was reduced to a few yards by whirling snow ; he had to rely to a certain extent on instinct and to a very great extent on sheer luck, as he continued on his way.

He now began to realize, however, that the struggle was nearing its end. The cold was tightening its grip upon him, and a feeling of numbness, starting at his feet and moving upward to his head, enveloped his whole body. In the pit of his stomach there was " a strange, stiff, lifeless feeling," but he still went on. " I remember," he writes, " struggling on and on for what seemed an interminable age, and of thinking dully what a useless business it was, how much easier to sit down and end it." [1] But mountaineers of Smythe's stamp just never do sit down and wait for death.

On and on he went. Suddenly he recognized on the North Ridge the broken ledge where he and Shipton had warmed themselves for a moment in the sun on the way up. One so rarely feels warm on Everest that such moments are never forgotten. He allowed himself to slide down on to the ledge, and as soon as he was below the ridge and sheltered from the wind he felt himself reviving. He clapped his hands together, and stamped his feet ; slowly and painfully the fatal numbness wore off, and the circulation returned to his ice-cold limbs. He realized then that the wind roaring a few feet above his head had been literally killing him by degrees.

When his strength was sufficiently restored he set off again. Although the hurricane had slackened off, the journey down still made painful demands on a man at the limit of his endurance.

Just as he approached Camp 5 he saw Shipton and Birnie leaving on their way down. He shouted to them to stop, but his hoarse voice would not carry ; the two men did not hear him, and calmly went on their way.

Smythe reached the camp to be faced with a fresh disappointment : the tents had been struck and could offer no shelter, not

[1] *Ibid.*, p. 214.

even for a short halt. Since there was nothing else for it, he went on towards the col, staggering along and constantly stopping, and sitting down as his legs gave way beneath him.

At last he was seen from the North Col, and Longland climbed a thousand feet to meet him with a Thermos-flask of hot and invigorating tea—so invigorating, in fact, that after drinking it Smythe completed the descent without any need of assistance.

A médical examination revealed him to be the only member of the assault parties to have returned without a temporarily enlarged heart. Yet he had had a weak heart as a boy, and at the age of twenty-seven had had to leave the Royal Air Force, his physique having proved inadequate. This will, I hope, give en couragement to boys who have ' overgrown their strength,' and who feel that they will never be fit for a life of adventure.

The altitude, however, still had some tricks up its sleeve, as the assault parties were to learn. On the following day they went down from the North Col with the support teams, and on meeting the contingent coming up towards them with supplies of hot tea Shipton discovered that he was incapable of expressing himself properly. When he tried to say, " Give me a cup of tea " he would say instead " tramcar " or " cat " or something equally preposterous. He knew very well what he wanted to say, but his tongue refused to say it. His companions looked at him with pity in their eyes, and in his exasperation he suddenly turned and made off down the glacier as fast as he could go. He arrived at Camp 3 well ahead of the rest, only to face another and quite unexpected ordeal —every one there was impatiently waiting for news of the assault. All he could get out, alas, was an incomprehensible humming and hawing, delivered, to make matters worse, in a confidential undertone, since he had still not recovered the full use of his voice.

After such an ambitious attempt on the summit the expedition might have been expected to turn back and give up the idea of conquering Everest that year. Nothing of the kind. After a week's rest at their base the climbers were already making fresh plans, despite the fact that the camp was situated in delightful surroundings where they might well have looked forward to a long stay. The June sun was hot, and the earth sweet-scented. Among the boulders there were poppies, gentians, primulas, and even a little grass. Best of all—the height of luxury—one could undress, and even wash ! Each of the 'sahibs' modestly retired to his personal tent for a bath, with the exception of three cold-water fiends who built a sort of swiming-pool filled with water from the glacier and plunged in—only to pop out, it is true, like corks from champagne-bottles !

On returning to Camp 3 they realized that the monsoon had

finally broken ; Everest was white from head to foot, and all chance of climbing it was gone. Until now they had hoped that by using their oxygen equipment this time they would be able to move up fast enough to make another attempt before the arrival of heavy snow. The breathing appliances had been considerably lightened, weighing no more than about fourteen pounds.

The equipment had not yet been used, partly on grounds of sportsmanship, but above all because since Norton's attempt the members of the expedition had firmly believed it possible, with proper training, to reach the summit without oxygen.

Now it was too late. Without even having tried their equipment out, they turned their backs on the mountain and came down in a mood of general disappointment.

It was as though the Great Peak, like a character in a fairy-tale, had ringed its brow in self-defence with a magic circle through which no man might pass. Three times the climbers had been halted at the same point as if they had struck an unseen obstacle. . . . And yet they were among the strongest and the bravest of all.

In all good fairy-tales there comes a time when the hero finds some way of breaking through the enchanted barrier. This tale is no exception to the rule, and we shall see how in the end the magic circle was broken, that circle which had so far prevented men from plucking the white flower of victory, the fairest flower of all.

A.J.V.

CHAPTER IX

SECRET MOUNTAINEERING, OR
THREE INNOCENTS ABROAD

ON three occasions in thirty-two years of Everest mountaineering
were there men misguided—and, indeed, crazy—enough to try to
climb the mountain alone, but for the aid of one or two porters.
The spring of 1934 saw the first of these ventures.

Maurice Wilson—British, and a former Army captain—was a
visionary who had evolved a theory entirely his own, holding that
any man who abstained from food for three weeks would purge
his system of all physical and moral impurity, and emerge from
his fast with powers renewed and increased. He had experienced

some sort of vision, and believed that his mission lay in the propagation of his doctrine throughout the world, to the great benefit of mankind. He estimated that the publicity which would accrue from a solo ascent of Everest would further his cause—and in this he was certainly right, for any announcement of a successful attempt of this sort could not have failed to cause a sensation ! He remained wholly undeterred by the fact that he had no experience of mountaineering, and knew nothing whatever about this mountain.

The first idea that occurred to him was to simplify the ascent by using an aeroplane in which he might land on the side of the mountain, high enough up to leave himself only a short climb on foot to the summit. With this in view he learnt to fly, bought a small plane, and took off for India in it. Unfortunately, on arrival at Purnea his plane was confiscated. Undismayed, he walked on to Darjeeling, and set about preparing a land assault, since use of the air was now denied him. He took so little trouble, however, to keep his plans secret that finally the authorities forbade him to make the attempt even on foot.

Thereupon he got into touch with two Sherpas who had taken part in the 1933 expedition, and who promised to smuggle him into Tibet. His story was that he was going tiger-hunting with a friend, whereupon, booking an hotel room for six months so that he could leave his luggage there under lock and key, he disappeared. He left Darjeeling by night, disguised as a Tibetan, and crossed the frontier without arousing the suspicion of the guards. Once in Tibet he reverted to European dress, but neither he nor his porters were required to explain their presence or doings. All his impedimenta were carried on the back of a single pony.

After walking for twenty-five days they reached Rongbuk. He paid a visit to the Chief Lama of the monastery, and, describing himself as one of the members of the 1933 expedition, he asked for part of the equipment deposited there by Ruttledge. Then he set off alone, naively convinced that three or four days would see him on the summit of Everest. He carried with him a small shaving-mirror with which to heliograph signals from the top as a proof that he had succeeded. Being trained to fast, he carried no food-supply apart from some rice-water ! Unfortunately, he failed to take account of the spring storms which occur daily on the Rongbuk Glacier in April, and which proved such a trial that, having reached the neighbourhood of Camp 2, he turned back and came down again. He allowed himself a fortnight's rest at Rongbuk, and then began to climb again with his three porters, reaching Camp 3 this time, and a height of 21,300 feet. There the porters showed him the store of food abandoned by Ruttledge. Presumably he did not relish his recollections of a rice-water diet, because despite his strict dietetic principles he took full advantage of the chocolate, Ovaltine, biscuits, and sardines left by the expedition.

We must assume too that he failed to inspire complete confidence in his Sherpas, since they refused to go beyond Camp 3. He ordered them, therefore, to wait a fortnight for him there, and pushed on alone, carrying a small, light tent with which he camped not far beyond the food-store. Arriving on the slopes of the North Col, he was most surprised not to find the steps cut in it by the previous year's expedition. Though armed with an ice-axe, he had no idea how to use it. He made his way farther up, came down again, and then started to climb once more. Day after day was consumed in fruitless efforts, yet he stuck to it, unwilling to renounce the goal he had set himself. Alas ! in spite of the food-supply at his disposal, his strength began to give out, and one day conditions at that altitude proved too much for him : while asleep in his tent he froze to death.

There he was found by Shipton the following year. His tent had been blown away, but the guy-ropes were still tied to the boulders holding them. Before they buried the poor fellow in a crevasse Shipton salvaged his note-book with the idea of finding out more fully what had happened.

The Sherpas maintained that they had waited a month for Wilson, but it is more likely that they made off down into the valley as soon as their supplies were exhausted, leaving this odd sahib, whose ways were so disquieting, to his lonely fate.

Later, in 1947, a Canadian called Denman emulated Wilson's exploit. With two Sherpas he left Darjeeling and entered Tibet under false pretences. Being luckier, and above all more competent, than his predecessor, he set up four successive camps, and struggled up above the North Col to a height of 24,000 feet, at which point cold and inadequate equipment forced him back.

Finally in 1951 came a Danish mountaineer, R. B. Larsen, to add his solo attempt on the North Face of Everest. Without permission, and without even a passport, he secretly reached the Tibetan side of the mountain by crossing Nepal. Thence with a few Sherpas he made his way up the North Col. At this height the porters refused to camp, as Larsen was not adequately equipped : he had not even a stove to cook his food ! The porters retraced their steps, heedless of the bitter reproaches of their sahib, who, happily less headstrong than Wilson, thereupon followed suit.

CHAPTER X

A LIGHT EXPEDITION

In 1934 Eric Shipton, accompanied by Tilman, had undertaken a private expedition to the Himalayas. The two climbers had explored the region of Nanda Devi, successfully climbed Trisul (22,700 feet), and crossed a good dozen cols.

These successes had convinced Shipton that light expeditions had a better chance than large-scale undertakings. We now know that in holding this theory he was misjudging the true state of affairs, but it must be admitted that at that time the unimpressive results obtained by the heavy expeditions appeared to justify his views.

He held that a light expedition had the advantage of costing infinitely less, of being more mobile, more able to live on the country, and employing only a limited number of pack-animals and porters. Indeed, the Tibetan authorities had come to view with alarm the phenomenon of whole populations deserting their work on the land and devoting themselves to transporting the material of the

G

Everest expeditions, for they saw that a risk of local famine during the following year was being run. Moreover, the considerable sums of money which the British left behind were having a deplorable effect on Tibetan morality.

Shipton maintained furthermore that the best team was the one in which each man was indispensable, and felt that he had every chance of being included one day in the assault parties. This was not true of the large teams, in which a certain competitive spirit always prevailed. "Only a saint," said Shipton, "could pluck from the depths of his heart the wish that his neighbour should fall ill and that he should take his place."

There had never been any need for more than four men to make up the assault parties, so why have such a large reserve of climbers ? By all means allow for wastage through non-acclimatization or illness, but not to the extent of three to one. Besides, the publicity which raged round big expeditions gave the climbers involved the impression that the eyes of the world were upon them, and, by thus limiting their freedom of judgment, lessened their chances of success.

Eric Shipton's ideas made such an impression on the organizers that in 1935 they decided to send a light expedition to Everest. It should be added that the permission of the Dalai Lama arrived too late that year to allow time for an official expedition to be arranged.

The object of this venture was to study weather and snow conditions on Everest during and after the monsoon, to train new men, make topographical surveys, and consider the possibilities of ascent on the south-western side. For the first time since 1921 there was once more a tendency to favour the south face of the mountain as offering an easier route than the north.

Eric Shipton was made responsible for the reconnaissance expedition, and took with him five climbers, a topographer, and fifteen hand-picked Sherpas.

Since it had to be on the mountain during and after the monsoon, the expedition set out later than its forerunners, and did not leave Darjeeling until May 24. Nor did it follow the recognized route, but instead hugged the southern frontier of Tibet, thus enjoying the luxury of playing truant in the neighbouring ranges.

In Tibet the expedition replenished its stock of food from local resources. Mutton, butter, yak's milk, and above all an abundance of eggs were easily obtained. The men consumed a stupendous quantity of the latter. Each ate on an average ten or fifteen a day, and one day four of them disposed of a hundred and forty. Shipton admitted that not all the eggs were quite fresh, and that they had to be scrambled or made into omelettes to allow the best to compensate for the more doubtful.

On July 4 the contingent arrived at Rongbuk with a clean bill of health ! Moving at remarkable speed, it reached Camp 3 in three days, and there came upon the body of poor Wilson.

The climbers then inspected the North Face of Everest, and were surprised to find it coated with white, and with few rocks showing. Yet when it had been observed a fortnight before from neighbouring peaks it had appeared dark-coloured and dry. Since then it had evidently received the first visits of the monsoon.

Under these circumstances it seemed advisable to attack the slopes of the North Col only with the greatest circumspection, since snow brought by the monsoon can be treacherous.

They climbed, suspicious and watchful, but saw nothing to cause anxiety ; not the tiniest crack, nor the slightest sign of loosening. With their fears thus allayed they and their porters tramped back and forth in the snow for three days while setting up the North Col camp.

Their object was to climb to some 26,000 feet by the orthodox route in order to learn what they could about the behaviour of the snow. The weather had for some time been perfect, with that alternation of warm days and cold nights ideal for firm settlement. If the snow had packed down properly on to the flat rocks, as one might hopefully expect, then the climb would be made very much easier. They were ready to strike when bad weather intervened, lasting four days. After that the climbers decided not to waste time waiting for the snow to harden, and abandoned the North Col for the time being. They were surprised on the way down to see that the blizzard had left no more than four to six inches of fresh snow on the slopes.

Having covered 200 feet at the most they were halted in their tracks by a huge gap. The slope had peeled off, leaving a step six feet deep and a quarter of a mile long. The avalanche must have fallen in the night, but no one had heard anything. They experienced retrospective qualms at the thought that this very snow had earlier seemed so firm that for three days they and the porters had cheerfully and continually tramped up and down over it !

A lively discussion thereupon ensued. Some wanted to climb back again. Shipton insisted on going on down, and finally had his way. He maintained quite soundly that within the avalanche-track nothing could shift again because it had all fallen as far as it could, and pointed out that if they waited a fresh fall might develop, involving very real danger. So they went on.

After this warning they readily agreed to abandon Everest. After all, they could study the quality of the snow on less dangerous mountains. So, with that delightful feeling of being on holiday, they turned their attention to other peaks.

During these later climbs they noticed that every time they climbed beyond 23,000 feet the consistency of the snow changed : whereas below this height it was firm, above it it never hardened, and remained treacherous, thus constituting a permanent source of difficulty. It became clear thereupon that the best time to attack Everest is at a season of relatively little snow. This meant a return to the traditional preference for the pre-monsoon period, when the rocks are dry because the winter winds have blown the snow from them.

This being established, the expedition decided to go off to explore the north-western approaches to the mountain. They split up into small groups, Shipton and Bryant going up the West Rongbuk Glacier as far as the snow-clad saddle reached by Mallory in 1921. Here they were able to confirm their predecessor's conclusion that any descent from there by the Khumbu Glacier is impossible. But Shipton saw enough of the West Cwm to make him want to investigate further in that direction some day.

Meanwhile Tilman and Wigram got to the Lho La Col. On the return they declared, as Bullock had done in 1921, that it was impassable, and that the lower part of the west ridge which joins it was quite unscaleable.

The expedition enjoyed itself for a few more weeks running up and down mountains, to such effect that it accounted in all for twenty-six new peaks of over 20,000 feet, not to mention the crossing of numerous cols.

A.J.V.

CHAPTER XI

THE SHERPAS

WITH his departure for the Nanda Devi close at hand, Eric Shipton was looking forward to the opportunity this light expedition would provide of gaining a more intimate knowledge of the Sherpas, a knowledge which over-large expeditions had ruled out. On his return he wrote :

> Sharing with them the same life, the same camp-fire, the same food and, later, the burden of load-carrying, we soon came to regard them as fellow-mountaineers rather than servants and they felt with us the excitement of anticipation and the joy of success. We were admitted to their endless jokes and their occasional philosophical talk. We relied upon their judgment as much as upon our own.[1]

To this he added the following eulogy :

> For unselfish loyalty, for strength and endurance, for sureness of foot and steadiness of head, for resourcefulness in all kinds of conditions, and as delightful companions, the best of them are unbeatable.[2]

[1] *Upon that Mountain*, p. 147.
[2] *Ibid.*, p. 149.

Yet Shipton recognized that among them, as among men everywhere, there are the good and the bad. Each individual has his qualities and defects. Some are good mountaineers but lack intelligence, others, more intelligent, break down under stress. Another may be a born leader but a bad climber. Then there are the shirkers, like the porter who ate a red sweet and then spat in the snow to persuade Ruttledge that his lungs were affected, and that he needed rest. There are also men like Tenzing, whose calibre as man and mountaineer singled him out at the critical moment to join Hillary in the last victorious assault.

The Sherpas have always shown complete loyalty to their white masters. Smythe relates that one morning he tried to come down from Camp 5 after a frightful storm, and, finding his hands frozen up to the wrist, had to creep back into the tent to give them a rub. He was on his knees weakly beating his palms together when a porter, noticing that he was in difficulties, slipped into the tent, grinned broadly, and set about massaging Smythe's hands in his own until the circulation was restored. Smythe was subsequently to learn that the poor fellow was himself suffering from severe frost-bite at the time.

And Birnie owed his life to Da Tsering on the day when, on his way down from Camp 5, he tried to slide on the snow, lost his footing, and toppled forward head first. Da Tsering, who was standing on a rock, did not hesitate a moment, but plunged down the slope, and luckily managed to stop the white man on a flat stretch of soft snow. He laughed loudly at the rescue as if it had been a great joke.

Yet the Sherpas' tendency to superstition sometimes leads them to behave in a quite inhuman fashion. On the North Col one of them became paralysed, and had to be carried. His closest friends refused to lift him on to their shoulders, and proposed to leave him there, maintaining that the mountain claimed a victim, and that if she were not satisfied she would wreak vengeance by striking down one of those responsible for cheating her of her due. Tilman was almost bursting with indignation at this, and it needed all his forcefulness to make their better selves prevail.

Born and bred in the uplands, the Sherpas are brought up from infancy to carry loads : hence, although not growing up into burly men, they become first-rate porters. They are rather short, but well-proportioned, nimble, and energetic. Living as they do in a rigorous climate, they stand up to the cold quite astonishingly. They are indefatigably active, and chatter away ceaselessly among themselves. " You wonder when they sleep," Ruttledge remarked.

They are cheerful and jolly, with a sense of humour and a

strong liking for practical jokes. "Each enjoyed jokes against himself as delightedly as those which he perpetrated. Two of them would conceal a heavy rock in the load of the third, and when, after an exhausting climb, this was discovered, all three would be convulsed with mirth." [1]

Being full of fun, they enjoy playing jokes on their masters. With long faces they came and told Tilman that they had eaten up all their food, and asked for an extra allowance to buy some more. When he granted their request, "Caught you!" they thundered delightedly.

They are also quite familiar up to a point, and irreverently christened one of the sahibs "Two Foot Six" on account of his diminutive size, and laughingly asserted that he never climbed to the same altitudes as the others.

They also had bets as to whether Finch or Mallory would climb highest on Everest. They love betting, and at the annual horse races at Darjeeling they may well put sums of money on a horse that are quite considerable, in relation to their meagre resources.

The Eastern Section of the Himalayan Club has done a great deal towards organizing the Sherpas, who are now given, in the same way as Alpine guides, a little book showing the expeditions in which they have taken part and their employers' estimate of their capabilities.

Some of the Sherpas are now such competent mountaineers that they are entrusted, even on difficult stretches, with the leadership of a roped party. Thus a cadre of professional climbers is being formed which may one day be expanded into a Company of Himalayan Guides. And it is possible that in the not too distant future the tourist may engage a Sherpa at the Guide Bureau of Darjeeling or Katmandu to climb a 23,000-foot peak just as easily as at Chamonix or Zermatt a guide is engaged for the Aiguille Verte or Monte Rosa.

[1] Shipton, *op. cit.*, p. 151.

A.J.V.

CHAPTER XII

THE ERA OF DISAPPOINTMENT

1936

THE 1936 expedition, placed once more under Ruttledge's leadership, was one of the strongest ever brought together. Unfortunately, the climbers were to have no opportunity of showing their capabilities for the monsoon arrived three weeks ahead of its normal date. It crossed the Indian plains in four days, faster than at any time in living memory, and broke over Everest, covering the mountain with fresh snow, so that little hope of success could be entertained. The North Col camp was established even so, but then abandoned. The members of the expedition wandered about for a few days on the Rongbuk Glacier, in enforced idleness, and at a loose end.

Finally, as the weather picked up a little, Shipton and Wyn Harris lost patience and resolved to climb back up to the North Col. "It was a ridiculous thing to do," Shipton said afterwards; and well he might, for about half-way up to the col the whole surface of the slope began to move down under him. He owed his life to his companion's nimbleness, for Harris dived back into a crevasse to belay him; and also to the fact that the avalanche stopped before the rope broke. After that they were wise enough not to persist in their efforts, and after a day or two the expedition was called off and they withdrew to Darjeeling.

1938

By 1938 financial difficulties were beginning to be felt. The papers had run out of stirring Everest news, and public

A. J. V.

interest started to flag. Money was no longer flowing into the coffers of the Everest Committee as it had done, and there was now no choice but to exercise economy and organize a light expedition at a smaller outlay. It was decided that in future members should pay their own quota to swell the total of grants received and subscriptions collected.

Tilman was appointed leader of the new expedition, and agreed to take on the responsibility because he regarded this as an enterprise of friends rather than as an official expedition. If it had not appeared to him in this light he would have refused, for he hated both the noisy publicity which surrounds large expeditions and the striking of heroic attitudes. " When our forerunners," he drily remarks, "were busy discovering the Alps, as we are now discovering the Himalaya, I feel sure they did not look upon themselves as so many bearded and bewhiskered embodiments of man's unconquerable spirit striving to attain the highest." [1]

The party chosen by him reached Rongbuk in early April, at which time the North Face of Everest looked promisingly black and free from snow. Camps 1 and 2 were established. Then, since the usual spring gales were blowing, and, moreover, the members were all suffering in a greater or less degree from throat troubles and colds, the party retired to the luxury of the Kharta Valley to nurse its ailments and wait for better conditions. But these, alas ! did not materialize. Gales were followed by hurricanes, and it was eventually realized that once more the monsoon had broken well ahead of normal schedule.

Returning from Kharta to Camp 3, they found the glacier covered with fresh snow a foot deep, and Everest white-clad like a bride. Though knowing full well that in such conditions there was no chance of reaching the summit, the party refused to face the facts. They tried hard to convince themselves that all was not lost, the wish being no doubt the father to the thought. Besides, they could hardly retreat without making at least an attempt. No sooner were hostilities joined than the North Col put its customary defensive measure into action, and released an avalanche beneath the feet of the first party, but fortunately it stopped before catastrophe occurred.

Twice the climbers reached the North Col, and twice they were forced down again by falls of snow. Discouraged by these setbacks, they turned their thoughts to the other side of the col, the west side. Despite what Mallory had said, it might very well, they thought, provide an easier approach than from the east, for, being

[1] H. W. Tilman, *Mount Everest, 1938* (Cambridge University Press, 1948), p. 108.

less exposed to the warm monsoon winds, it ought to be less subject to avalanches. Mallory, however, had not been mistaken, as every one realized as soon as they set foot on the slope, for it swept up steeply and regularly, being at no point sufficiently level to halt even the slightest slipping of the surface. Moreover, it was threatened from two sides : by the North Peak and by the North Face of Everest. Also from a large part of the surface an enormous avalanche had stripped off, leaving bare ice, so the party felt extremely relieved when they finally arrived on the North Col.

The next day they attacked the Ridge, and with a determined effort set up Camp 5, followed by Camp 6 at 27,200 feet. Smythe and Shipton spent the night in a spot with which they were familiar, and which they described as the most desolate on earth. They slept better than in 1933, but set off too early the following morning, before the sun had reached the North Face. Consequently no sooner did they plunge into the morass of powdery snow than their feet and hands lost all feeling. They were forced back into their tent to warm themselves for a little while, then set out again, but with no more success. They encountered snow hip-deep, and ploughed forward leaving a veritable trench in their wake. After an hour's exhausting toil they had not gone more than a rope-length, in spite of the fact that they were in an area of easy rocks. They persevered none the less ; but when the rocks steepened they realized that they were climbing beyond all limits of safety. The thick layer of snow masking the slabs might at any moment give way and carry them off. So they gave it up, feeling terribly dis-appointed, because on no previous occasion had they felt in such fine form at this stage. The following day Tilman and Lloyd had a similar experience, trying three or four sections above Camp 6, and each time, despite the fact that the climb appeared at first sight possible, not to say easy, being forced down by loose snow.

Back at Camp 3 the advisability of an autumn attempt was discussed. There were people in England who maintained that October and November, with their periods of clear days, would be as favourable for an ascent as May. But Smythe rightly pointed out that the North Face gets less sunlight at the later period, and that the intense cold would rule out any ascent in the shadow. Since every one agreed, it was decided to abandon the attempt for that year.

At Rongbuk monastery the Chief Lama gave them a huge meal, which the whole party devoured greedily. The eighth helping of macaroni in sauce finally dispelled the memory of the diet which

Tilman had imposed throughout the expedition as a healthy mountaineering regimen.

At the end of the meal the monks, who had learnt that the British could sing, asked to be treated to a sample of their talent. The visitors struck up a hymn, after which they were requested to put the sacred formula " Om Mani Padme Hum " to music, and complied with a successful adaptation of *God save the King* !

The use of oxygen had been much debated before the expedition set out ; Tilman was strongly opposed to it, urging tradition and the mountaineering code. He thought its use unsportsmanlike, and even unfair, as it created such artificial conditions that with it the term mountaineering ceased to be an honest description. Why not go on and enlist the aid of a kite ? " We must abide by the rules," declared Tilman, and his fulminations set alight once more the frightful row about artificial aids.

Smythe and Shipton too were opponents of oxygen. Shipton stressed that, as the apparatus contained only a limited supply of gas, if the ascent took longer than expected (which was quite likely), the climber ran a risk of suffocation on exhausting his supply.

The champions of oxygen—and there were some—were not all young mountaineers. In an article on this question Captain Farrar, president of the Alpine Club in 1926, had written : " This objective, the conquest of the mountain, must be kept steadily in view, and its attainment be attempted . . . *with every available resource.*" [1]

The 1938 expedition included two advocates of oxygen : Peter Lloyd and Warren. They had two types of apparatus at their disposal. One had a closed circuit, the wearer breathing pure oxygen through a mask covering his nose and mouth. The other was an older and simpler open type, using a mixture of oxygen and air.

The objection to the first type was that it weighed thirty-five pounds and contained only four hours' supply of oxygen. The other was that used by Finch's expedition in 1922 ; its oxygen capacity was double that of the first type, it weighed fifteen pounds less, it had no mask, and its simpler working made it less liable to go wrong.

Warren tried the closed-circuit type above the North Col, but soon had to take off the mask, as it was suffocating him. Lloyd then tried it, with exactly the same result. But the air-mixture apparatus he found beneficial when he had discovered the knack of breathing with it, which entailed biting the rubber tube to stop

[1] Quoted in Tilman, *op. cit.*, p. 108.

the arrival of oxygen while breathing out, and releasing it while breathing in.

With this apparatus he reached Camp 6 and, with Tilman, tried to get up on the North Face. He believed that oxygen had kept him free from distress and feeling continually fit. However, Tilman did not use it, and was going equally well beside him, so the experiment produced no conclusive evidence in favour of oxygen.

For some time thenceforth Everest was to go unmolested. Its attackers went forth to fight other battles, to defend their soil, their rights, and their liberties, including the liberty to take their pleasure as they willed. While they strove the great mountain was restored to its pride and its peace. Its life went on. The dawns cast their hues upon it, the evening suns set it aglow, and the nights never wholly quenched its whiteness. Down its sides the glaciers wound ; at its feet crevasses gaped. Ice gleamed, and snow swirled and coiled around it.

And no man was there to wonder at its splendour. But mountains have no need of man ; they offer their beauty for their own delight.

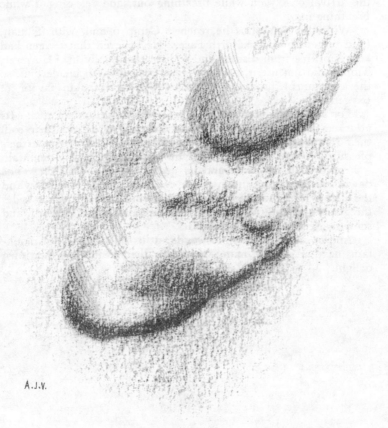

A.J.V.

CHAPTER XIII

THE ABOMINABLE SNOWMAN

His tracks are all we have for reconstructing his physical appearance, for he plays the Invisible Man and no European has ever seen him.

Is this sufficient reason for doubting his existence? Did not the men of the Kon-Tiki expedition teach us that there are creatures in the sea which no one had hitherto set eyes on, thus confounding those who believe that science has arrived at final knowledge concerning the world of living things? If the sea contains creatures unknown to us, why should not the loftier regions of our globe harbour beasts of unknown species ? The fact that Europeans have never beheld the Snowman means nothing. So far there have been comparatively few expeditions to the Himalayas, and vast tracts of mountain ranges remain unexplored still.

We know that the people of the region never venture on to the glaciers except to follow traditional routes over the chain via the high passes. Nevertheless, many a Tibetan and Sherpa has seen the Snowman, which proves that this fabulous creature, normally confined to the higher altitudes like the chamois in the Alps, does sometimes—again like that animal—descend to milder regions in search of food.

Although there is no reason to doubt that Tibetans and Sherpas have actually seen the Abominable Snowman, it must be admitted that the description they give of it is so fantastic that a certain reserve and scepticism are justified. The *yeti*, as the Sherpas call it, is said to be six feet six inches tall, and prodigiously powerful. The joints of its knees and elbows are reversed, and its toes point backward. (The former detail is rather amusing, for what climber during the ascent of some steep, snow-clad slope has not wished he could reverse the joints of those knees that stub the rock-face and throw him off his balance ?) It is a shaggy creature, and as it goes downhill its long, matted hair tumbles over its eyes, preventing it from seeing. For that reason the best course, on coming face to face with it, is to run away down the mountain, for it will attack man. It is extremely fierce, and feeds on yak and human flesh. Here we have indeed a genuine ogre, the terror of old and young alike !

The fact is, however, that Europeans let their imagination run away with them as much as the natives when they try to picture the Snowman. He has been likened in turn to wolf, bear, otter, elephant, leopard, monkey, and man !

Whatever the truth may be, taking all evidence into consideration, it is surprising how often the tracks of the *yeti* have been encountered.

The expedition of 1921 was the first to discuss the creature. It will be recalled that the Lama of Rongbuk monastery warned the members of the expedition that five Abominable Snowmen haunted the glacier basin. Nevertheless, neither Europeans nor porters ever saw tracks on the glacier. It seems likely that the wretched creatures were terrified by the influx of this begoggled host, and thereupon emigrated to other places in the vicinity, since it was in the snows of Lhakpa La that Howard-Bury found the tracks which so puzzled him in 1921. They resembled human

footprints, and although the porters unhesitatingly identified them
as belonging to the *yeti*, Howard-Bury was more disposed to conclude
that " these tracks . . . were probably caused by a large ' loping '
grey wolf, which in the soft snow formed double tracks rather like
those of a barefooted man." [1]

Curiosity was generally aroused, and some one suggested the
following explanation : these were the footprints of a malefactor.
Capital punishment does not exist in Tibet ; instead delinquents
are in some cases banished from villages or monasteries to wander
at large in search of their food. Yet it was not clear what sustenance
any evil-doer might hope to find 20,000 feet up on a glacier.
Alternatively, perhaps, there were hermits living in the seclusion
of the mountains. But it seemed surprising that one of these holy
men should add to his daily mortifications, great enough in all
conscience, that of taking walks barefoot in the snow.

In 1936 the Snowman was again in the news. A traveller
declared that in the high Brahmaputra valley, at an altitude of
some 16,000 feet, he had come upon " five sets of tracks which
looked exactly as though made by a barefooted man." [2] This
statement was followed by a similar one from another explorer
who had seen comparable tracks near the source of the Ganges.

Had they been made by some animal, such as a langur monkey ?
Much argument ensued. Unfortunately, this variety of large
monkey does not walk on its hind legs, and lives in trees. Could
it be a panda, then ? But the panda has small feet with claws,
and lives exclusively on bamboo shoots, which do not grow in the
neighbourhood of glaciers.

In 1937 Smythe and his Sherpas were on a col of the central
Himalayas at a little over 16,000 feet when they discovered " the
imprints of a huge foot, apparently of a biped." [3] Again the porters
diagnosed the tracks of the Snowman. Smythe acted with scientific
precision, measuring and photographing them, and then sending
his findings on to British zoologists, who declared that without a
shadow of doubt the tracks were those of a bear, *Ursus arctos
pruinosus*.

The authorities having pronounced their verdict, the question
seemed settled. But far from it ! For next a traveller who had
returned from the Himalayas told how in the Karakoram mountains
at the west end of the range he had seen tracks which were " roughly
circular, about a foot in diameter, nine inches deep and eighteen

[1] C. K. Howard-Bury, *Mount Everest : The Reconnaissance, 1921* (Arnold, 1922),
p. 141.
[2] Tilman, *Mount Everest, 1938*, Appendix B, p. 130.
[3] *Ibid.*, p. 131.

South of the Khumbu Glacier : Kangtega

inches apart. They lay in a straight line without any right or left stagger, nor was there any sign of overlap as would be the case with a four-footed beast." [1] The traveller in question took photographs, but, being less competent than Smythe, took two on the same film, and thus rendered his evidence useless.

Then—heaven knows why !—the theory that it might be an otter was being considered, when somebody declared that on a glacier of the Garwhal mountains he had found tracks " which resembled nothing so much as those of an elephant." [2] But he admitted that it was not likely to have been one, as these pachyderms were somewhat rare in the Himalayas. Indeed, even the enterprising elephant of Kipling's little Toomai, setting forth at dead of night, and betaking itself to the sacred dance performed annually by the beasts of the elephant tribe, would surely have shunned such a route.

With a whole menagerie of animals thus invoked, it is difficult to imagine what the Snowman can really look like, unless indeed it resembles a man ; but an unclean man, for the adjective the Tibetans use has the meaning of ' filthy ' or ' disgusting,' no less than that of ' monstrous ' or ' horrifying.' Indeed, people began to get excited at the prospect of discovering a kind of sub-man, a crude, primitive archetype of humanity providing the missing link in the chain of creatures from the beasts to *Homo sapiens*.

In 1938 Tilman, while climbing up the Zemu glacier, in the Kanchenjunga range, spotted a relatively recent trail at about 19,000 feet. It went up, across the col, and then disappeared among the rocks on the other side. Tilman had been under the impression that he was the first to go that way, and was furious at having been forestalled. Back at Darjeeling he took steps to find out who had beaten him to it, but to his surprise learnt that no one had been anywhere near there. Now, in the Himalayas a roped party cannot pass unobserved ; it requires porters, and porters talk. They are the sources of news about mountain happenings.

Then Tilman discovered that the year before a similar mystery had puzzled a British major at the same spot. He too found tracks—double ones, this time—on the final slope of the Zemu Gap. Over a certain distance, moreover, they appeared to consist of steps actually cut. At first the major assumed that they had been left by a German party which had been mountaineering in the district for some time. But on investigation it was discovered that the Germans had at no time climbed in that vicinity.

[1] Quoted by Tilman, *op. cit.*, p. 132.
[2] *Ibid.*, p. 133.

The cut steps were most surprising, and seemed to indicate that the creature responsible for them was endowed with a certain amount of intelligence. The question also arose whether it might have been able to construct some kind of snow-shoe—which would have accounted for the circularity of the tracks—or whether, finding climbing-boots discarded by some expedition on a moraine, it might have thought of putting them on to help itself along !

Fresh evidence in support of the theory of a quasi-human Snowman was then forthcoming. A book appeared telling of the strange experiences of a certain explorer. In the selfsame Zemu region he had caught sight of something rather like a human form three hundred yards away :

> It was going upward at walking pace, occasionally stopping to pull up young dwarf rhododendron shrubs. The figure stood out black against the snow and wore no clothing. A minute later it plunged into a thicket and vanished. . . . Its tracks, similar in shape to human footprints, measured six or seven inches in length, nine inches in width and were twelve to eighteen inches apart. The marks of the five toes and the instep were clear, but not that of the heel.

Yet " no man had been in this direction since the beginning of the year."

During the War no one worried about the creature, and it could roam unmolested in these altitudes between 13,000 and 17,000 feet which seem to be its natural habitat. But in 1951 there was news of it again.

While crossing the Menlung La pass, in the Gaurisankar range, Eric Shipton discovered unfamiliar marks in the snow. They were double, showing that at least two creatures had passed that way. Shipton sent a report on this to *The Times* : .

> The tracks had mostly been blurred by the thaw into oval imprints, slightly longer and much wider than those left by our big climbing boots. But here and there where the snow covering the ice was thin, we came upon a well-preserved footprint of the creature. It showed three toes and a big toe of great size. One point was particularly interesting. The tracks crossed a crevasse and it was obvious that the creature had leapt across and used its toes to gain a foothold in the snow on the other side.

The nail-marks were still visible. Murray and Bourdillon noticed them when they too saw the tracks a few days later while crossing the col. " We followed the tracks," Shipton went on,

> for nearly two miles down the glacier to where the ice is covered with moraine deposits. I had in the past encountered many of these strange
> H*

tracks in various parts of the Himalayas and in the Karakoram, but I
had never before found any so well preserved.

Some of these tracks still showed the lines on the sole of the foot
delicately imprinted in the snow, which proved how recent was
the spoor. Shipton and his porters can only just have missed
seeing the Abominable Snowman and his mate that day. The
latter may for all we know have been watching from some rocky
hiding-place as the men examined their footprints.

Sen Tenzing and the porter who were with Shipton immediately
identified the tracks as those of *yetis*. Sen Tenzing claimed to have
seen a Snowman in the neighbourhood of Thyangboche monastery
at the time of a religious festival. Under cover of trees the *yeti*
had come to within twenty yards or so of the assembled pilgrims,
and many had caught a glimpse of the creature. Sen Tenzing
described it as semi-human, semi-animal, about five feet six inches
in height, its body covered with reddish-brown hair, but hairless
on the face.

At any rate, whatever it is, the *yeti* exists, and we can be sure
that one day Europeans will run across it. It is probably a peace-
loving, herbivorous creature feeding on roots and young shoots.
We certainly know that it is a shy one, and it is perhaps after all
to be congratulated on the good sense it has so far shown in keeping
clear of the white man, for it will, one fears, suffer capture or death
when either curiosity or bad luck one day brings it out of its shell.

PART II: EVEREST FROM THE SOUTH

CHAPTER XIV

THE 1951 RECONNAISSANCE

WHEN the world finally emerged from the frightful upheaval of the Second World War mountaineers recalled that they had not done with Everest, and that an old score had still to be paid off.

Since 1938 the political situation in Asia had changed, and the Communist invasion of Tibet had closed the northern line of access. Fortunately, while one door closed another opened : Nepal waived its objections, and offered the Europeans free passage over its territory. The southern slopes of Everest were now open to attack.

In 1950 Tilman and Houston went to look round. They travelled up the Khumbu glacier, and from there, cutting westward, reached the lower slopes of Pumori, which enabled them to look along that deep and mysterious valley below the West Ridge which Mallory named the West Cwm (see map, p. 154). No encouraging conclusions could be drawn from their observations : the way into the West Cwm was blocked by an ice-fall, so that it seemed almost inaccessible, while the slope of the South Col [1] appeared to lack that absolute necessity, a potential camp site.

Despite these unfavourable reports, a British reconnaissance expedition was launched in 1951 under Eric Shipton, the man who knew Everest best, and included Murray, Bourdillon, Michael Ward, Riddiford, and, for the first time, Hillary. The expedition's departure was delayed by difficulties in getting the party together, and a start was not made until August 23, when the monsoon was at its height.

Whereas the northern route via Tibet winds through poor, arid country, wind-swept and sun-parched, the southern route through Nepal is over wooded hills and sheltered, cultivated lands where life is pleasanter.

This route involved the expedition in repeated climbs and descents, up over high passes, and down once more into valleys. It rained a great deal, but thanks to Angtharkay—the leader of the Sherpas with the French expedition to Annapurna—not once did they have to pitch a tent at night. This resourceful and loyal Nepalese got local people to put them up. The British never thought twice about exchanging their damp tent for a loft or a berth in the cow-shed, even cheek-by-jowl with a calf. For, in the words of that fanatical Alpine camper Daniel Souverain, "A tent is nice, but not as nice as a good stone house with a roof."

[1] The north, south, and west cols round Everest should be called Chang La, Lho La, and Nup La respectively, since in Tibetan *chang* means north, *lho* south, and *nup* west. However, the West Col was christened Lho La by Mallory when he discovered it in 1921, and the name has stuck. If it were changed now a great deal of confusion would arise, as has happened in similar cases in the Alps, where people have tried to rename places in the Mont Blanc massif. We do not, therefore, feel entitled to begin correcting a system of place-names established through thirty-two years of use. Hence we shall continue to refer to the western col of Everest as Lho La, using the English designation South Col for the genuine southern pass.

On arrival at Sola Khumbu, the Sherpas' home country, progress slowed down almost to a standstill on account of *chang* (home-brewed beer)

and *rakhsi*, another home-made alcoholic drink. The porters drank large quantities of these beverages with friends whom they had in every village—and the villages were strung out along the whole length of the Dudh Kosi valley.

Despite all this the expedition arrived in the Khumbu basin on September 29 and pitched its Base Camp on the glacier at 18,000 feet. Now the ice-fall could be seen, and looked even more awe-inspiring than they had imagined. It was 2000 feet high, and seen from below it was as if this colossal heap of ice had been disgorged from the mouth of a giant. It consisted of huge, towering blocks as thick as houses and packed close together, having straddled and somersaulted over each other down to the bottom, and then been forced back up again and ground away by the pressure of ice. At the mouth of the Cwm fresh accumulations continually threatened to collapse and swell the mass.

The very day after arriving, the party set out for the assault. They noticed to their left a kind of corridor made by the débris of successive avalanches running along the foot of Everest's western spur. The crevasses there, filled up with ice and snow, would have provided an easy way, but the area was very dangerous, and there would have been no sense in choosing any route there which would have to be walked over continually by porters.

They therefore tried to find a way through towards the middle of the glacier. On the first day they got half-way up the ice-fall ; and on the second, by using the old steps, they were quickly up to the point reached the day before. Beyond it they wound their way through a maze of seracs and crevasses, and though they sank deeply into the snow they nevertheless persevered. They were nearly at the top when Shipton remarked, " This snow looks likely to avalanche ! " And straight away, as if the slope had been waiting to confirm his words, it broke away, carrying Riddiford with it. Fortunately, the rope held him, upside down, at the edge of a crevasse. He was pulled back, and they stopped to recover their breath, by which time it was getting late, so they went no farther that day.

After that hair-raising episode they left the Khumbu glacier and explored the mountains near by. On their return they noticed that there had been a great upheaval in the ice-fall. Over a wide area the seracs were smashed up and chasms opened, with shattered ruins of ice-blocks precariously balanced on the edge of them.

Hillary prepared nevertheless to cross this chaos ; but the first block he tackled collapsed with an awful roar, shaking the whole glacier as if an earthquake had struck it. The porters threw themselves to the ground in terror.

Clearly further collapse was to be feared. They looked for a better way to the right, but found only an even wider shattered area than the first, so they turned back. Being resolute men, they were not disheartened by these failures. They waited a day or two and then returned in force—all six of them, with three porters —and this time the change in the seracs considerably improved matters. The blocks had locked together and formed bridges over the crevasses. The climbers zig-zagged back and forth, and then split up and attacked three different sections. After an hour it was learnt that Bourdillon had found the best way along an ice-ridge, so they all followed him, and eventually their efforts were rewarded : they emerged where the glacier flattened out.

But the way was not yet clear. They had moved forward only a short distance when they encountered the biggest crevasse they had ever set eyes on. At its narrowest point it was a hundred feet across, and at its widest a hundred yards. It was incredibly deep, and, what was worse, it split the glacier from Everest to Nuptse ! There was no way of turning it on the right. On the left it might possibly be crossed by the snow-corridor, but it would be madness to attempt it. Defeated in the very moment of what had seemed to be victory, the party returned to camp, dispirited, and wondering whether any reasonable route could ever be found over this awesomely turbulent glacier.

CHAPTER XV

THE SWISS EXPEDITIONS OF 1952

The Planning Stage

So far it had been accepted among mountaineers that Everest was an exclusively British preserve. The work they had put in towards its conquest, spread over nine expeditions, in a way justified the monopoly, but it was unfortunate that other eligible climbers were thereby deterred from making an attempt.

There was another reason for their hesitation. The British, having been for long the ruling power in India, had undertaken a number of expeditions to the Himalayas during which sound experience of high-altitude climbing had been obtained. Foreign mountaineers were apprehensive of tackling so formidable a task as the ascent of Everest without similar knowledge behind them, for fear of not being up to it and making a poor show.

The Swiss, however, had three successful Himalayan expeditions to their credit, those of 1947, 1948, and 1950, and had lost their inferiority complex. They therefore decided to ask the Nepalese Government for permission to try from its territory.

They then learnt that the British were also planning an attempt from the south that very year. So, to make everybody happy, and since there was every wish to co-operate on both sides, an Anglo-Swiss expedition was talked of. But at the London meetings held to discuss the project no agreement could be reached on the difficult and delicate question as to whether a Swiss or an Englishman should lead the party. Collaboration then fell through, and it was decided that the Swiss, whose preparations were already well advanced, should make an attempt in 1952, and the British in 1953.

It was in the small, closed circle of the Androsace Club of Geneva that the idea of an Everest expedition had taken shape. The Androsace is a club of fanatical mountaineers, who spend all their holidays climbing, and who, every week-end, scale peaks on skis or on foot, using any bit of free time for training on the rocky cliffs of the Salève. The Chamonix folk are well acquainted with this group of Geneva friends, who every Saturday happily invade the mountain huts of the Mont Blanc massif, turning in often enough at eleven o'clock at night, after climbing high peaks, and setting out again early on Sunday morning.

It was no problem to pick out the members of the expedition from these enthusiasts, who all knew each other well, and had been climbing together for years. Their comradeship was certainly a great factor in welding the party into a team, although naturally it was not free from the inevitable disagreements that arise in all expeditions. We understand, for example, that Dittert complained of Lambert's inordinate liking for jam, and that Roch and Hofstetter quarrelled at one awkward moment, yet it can be confidently stated that there was never a happier and more united body of climbers. The Swiss were uniquely fortunate in being able to bring together an expedition on an ' all-friends-together ' basis.

The party under the leadership of Dr Wyss-Dunant consisted of Asper, Aubert, Dr Chevalley, Dittert (leader of the assault parties), Flory, Hofstetter, Lambert, and Roch, with the scientists Lombard and Zimmermann, a geologist and a botanist respectively. Some of them, Roch, Dittert, Chevalley, and Wyss-Dunant, had already had some experience of the Himalayas. Lambert was a mountain guide with innumerable feats of Alpine skill and endurance to his credit. His performance on Everest was a triumph of mind over matter, for he had previously been partially disabled while climbing.

In February 1937, during the first winter ascent of the Aiguille du Diable, with two climbers who were employing him (one of them a woman), he was caught in a storm on the ridges between Mont Maudit and Mont Blanc du Tacul. Since they were not able to come down, the three of them had to spend four nights at a temperature of $-40°$ F. On the fifth day, in order to save his charges, Lambert set off alone into the Combe Maudite to seek help. He was unsteady on his feet, for he had eaten nothing for several days, and his feet felt like lead and were frost-bitten, as he had given his socks to the young woman. When the rescue parties met him on their way up the glacier he collapsed. He was suffering from such severe frost-bite that all his toes had to be amputated. When he again stood up and attempted to walk he fell forward at every step he tried to take, and it seemed clear that his mountaineering days were over. But he refused to be beaten, and patiently set about overcoming his handicap. He taught himself to walk again with the aid of specially made shoes, and in time managed to resume his livelihood as a guide, since when he has done climbs as exacting as before. What would he have said if some one had told him, as he was being carried on a stretcher down the Mer de Glace, that one day he would be climbing near the summit of Everest?

The members of the party each paid their own financial contribution to the general expenses of the expedition, and, helped by the Swiss Foundation for Alpine Research, they had no difficulty in raising the remainder of the necessary funds.

The question of equipment was studied with characteristic Swiss care, method, and eye for the serviceable, good-quality article. Nothing was spared to fit out the expedition with the best of every requirement.

Novelties were : untanned reindeer-skin boots like those worn by Eskimos and Lapps, felt and down slippers, fur caps, double silk gloves, down mitts, nylon cagoules with double thickness of silk, and canvas shoe-bags completely enveloping the boot, sole and all.

They took flags and wooden pegs to mark out routes, a walkie-talkie radio set, rockets, Bengal lights, various kinds of signal detonators, and explosives to set off avalanches.

In the matter of provisions a substantial proportion consisted of fruit juices. Their weight was no doubt a major drawback, but their high vitamin content made them a valuable food.

They had also oxygen apparatus of the so-called ' closed circuit ' type, from which the climber breathes pure oxygen.

Needless to say, they had met together many times to study thoroughly the southern route and discuss its possibilities. Information had been provided by Tilman and Shipton, who had, more-over, obligingly put at their disposal a fine photograph of the Khumbu glacier basin.

The Approach through Nepal

Bombay. Delhi. By successive flight-stages the Swiss arrived one fine March day at Katmandu, the capital of Nepal. Some excitement was caused as they landed, for the plane touched down, then rose again unsteadily, and finally came down with a bump. It had evidently had to jump over a cow crossing the airfield in serene and confident awareness of the respect paid in India to its sacred person.

Nepal, with Tibet, is the highest country in the world, and contains eight of the fourteen loftiest peaks on earth. Its territory, 525 miles long and varying in breadth from 90 to 140 miles, is inhabited by seven million people, Hindus in the south, Buddhists in the north.

Katmandu (4450 feet) is surrounded by wooded hills over-topped by high, snowy peaks, and is reached only by air or on foot. Yet motor-cars are to be seen in the town, and lorries lumber about the outskirts. These vehicles have been carried here bodily on men's backs, not in parts to be assembled ! Secured, without their wheels, on large platforms, they have been borne over tracks impassable for motor traffic by fifty or sixty coolies marching in time to a song and carrying their load over passes 6500 feet high.

The town has a great many temples and pagodas, with their shining gold and silver roofs rising one above the other into the bright sky. The squat little houses have no panes of glass in their windows, but only delicately coloured curtains, and their woodwork is sometimes elaborately and ornately carved.

The streets of Katmandu, as of all Oriental towns, are very much alive. The men run about barefoot, carrying their loads at each end of a bamboo pole, the women spin, the children play, and people ply their many trades : tinkers, tailors, barbers, cobblers, and fish-friers. And in the midst of this hive of activity the ubiqui-tous cows stroll nonchalantly hither and thither, occasionally picking a vegetable from a stall, while women pass by, graceful in their long shawls and silver bracelets, and with flowers stuck in their coils of black hair.

There was no repeat performance here of Lambert's adventure in a Bombay bazaar. A cheapjack was pestering him, with that Oriental persistence that nothing can shake off. He was offering

a tiger's tooth which he was intent on selling, and which he shook
in the face of his prospective customer. This had been going on
for some time when Lambert, beside himself with exasperation,
suddenly had a brilliant idea. He pulled a false tooth out of his
mouth and shook it in the face of the hawker, who fled in terror !

At Katmandu the Swiss picked up their Sherpas. They were
delighted to renew acquaintance with Tenzing, who had been with
Dittert in 1947, and who was to lead the Sherpas on this occasion.
The members spent a day making odd purchases, cashing their
travellers' cheques, and straightening out mail problems with the
post-office. Finally they set out on March 29.

While Dittert was fascinated by the feet of the Sherpas, unshod,
nimble, and well arched, the natives for their part seemed intrigued
by Lambert's. "They must think shoes are heavy on the feet
when they look at me ! " he remarked good-humouredly. And,
indeed, his feet, which leave tracks as broad as the *yeti*'s, put the
finishing touch to a general appearance which has earned him
the nickname "Ourson" ("Bear Cub"). Strangely enough, the
porters too dubbed him "Bhalu sahib "—"Mr Bear."

On their way the Swiss passed through villages whose names
remained a mystery, since signposts have not yet grown up on
Nepalese roads. They passed peasants bound for Katmandu market
to sell their squawking fowls, women going to the temple carrying
copper plates laden with offerings to the gods : rice, herbs, tiny
cups, and rhododendron flowers. On their way back these women
would throw the remainder of their rice to the birds which rained
down in flocks around them.

They passed lorries too, which nearly choked them with dust.
Their metallic clatter was the parting shot of a receding civilization ;
soon only the sounds of the advancing party would be heard :
songs, laughter, talk, the shouts of passing children, and the patter
of bare feet on the dusty way. For a time, too, the roar of torrents,
and afterwards, nothing. "Throughout our approach journey,"
Dittert wrote, " we moved daily towards a silence ever purer and
more profound." [1]

The Swiss did not follow the same route as Shipton (see map
opposite) ; theirs ran from west to east, and involved more crossing
of hill and dale than the British had had to face. Dittert's impression
was that " the hand which fashioned the world's loftiest mountain
lost patience as it worked, and rumpled the earth around into an
angry frown." [2]

As in Sikkim, there is rich and abundant vegetation on the

[1] Dittert, *Avant-premières à l'Everest*, p. 24.
[2] *Ibid.*, p. 25.

south slopes of Everest. The trees are huge : tulip-trees with blood-red blossoms, walnuts, fig-trees with trunks over fifty feet in circumference. Then there are daturas, tree-ferns, garlands of orchids hanging from the branches of oaks, sweet-scented black and yellow jasmine, banana-trees, rich flamboyants, and, most conspicuous of all, giant rhododendrons with white, red, and pink blossoms which the Sherpas eat as Europeans eat acacia and nasturtium leaves. The wild flora of the Himalayas seems to be offered in a great basket of flowers.

In order to do a little modest farming for their living, however, the natives have had to reclaim land from all this over-exuberant natural growth, by setting fire to the forest and then cutting terraces up the steep slopes, so that these steps, as seen from a distance and thrown into relief by light and shade, make the hills look like the striped backs of huge zebras.

Often the Swiss would pitch their camp on one of these terraces, which give the effect of balconies overlooking the surrounding country. Wisely they decided to change sleeping-partners every night to avoid any forming of cliques, and also to ensure that the snorers went the rounds quite fairly !

Down in the valleys they sometimes had to cross rivers by alarmingly flimsy footbridges, or by rickety suspension bridges made of no more than a plank held up by chains. The remarkable thing was how well the heavily laden porters (among whom were women and boys) managed to keep their balance on them.

One morning, as the party was about to set off, one of the porters, a boy of sixteen, began to weep because his feet ached, though he refused to abandon his load. So Tenzing generously relieved him of a large part of it, leaving him only thirty-five pounds to carry. Generally the coolies carry seventy to eighty-five pounds, and some nearly as much as a hundred and forty pounds. When Dittert tried to shoulder a Sherpa's average load he found that the narrow straps cut into his shoulders, the bottom corners of the pack dug painfully into his back, and the front strap pulled on his neck muscles unbearably. So, to the great joy of the Sherpas, he dumped the load on the ground.

One day the party engaged a whole family : father, mother, and son of ten years, who, besides his load, carried a three-months-old brother. Before the departure they were able to observe the curious way in which this particular mother fed her baby. She chewed pellets of *tsampa* until they became soaked in saliva, and then transferred them directly from her mouth to the infant's, patting its stomach to help down the indigestible food. Evidently it is such primitive infant welfare that breeds in the Sherpa race

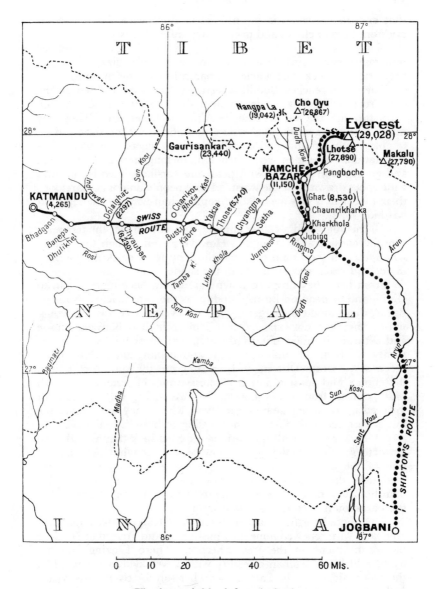

The Approach March from the South

Broken line : Shipton's route.
Continuous line : the Swiss Expedition's route.

that endurance which is the marvel of Europeans, for it is a far cry from here to clinics and proprietary infant foods !

Now that the ground was getting higher, the Swiss could see impressive mountains showing up in the north : dizzy faces and projections of rock, and glaciers apparently hanging in mid-air.

They then reached Buddhist territory, and were greeted on the outskirts of villages by the deep note of the long Tibetan horn, which rings through the valleys like its Alpine counterpart. They saw masts flying prayer-flags, *chortens* (monuments to the dead), dark temples with red-and-gold Buddhas smiling sleepily in silent contemplation. The men wear their hair in long tresses like women, and go about in felt caps with peak and ear-flaps lined in fur, and wide robes drawn in at the waist. These people do not go barefoot ; their footwear is of woven fabric coming half-way up the leg, and has hide soles.

All this suggested a colder climate, and now in fact the temperature fell considerably at night. However, even though they found white frost on their tents each morning, by ten o'clock the thermometer had risen to over 90° F. in the shade.

From here they dropped down again, and once more began to climb, and at noon on Easter Sunday, as they approached Namche Bazar, they caught their first glimpse of Everest. It was a dazzling sight ; they had not expected it to look so high ! Between Lhotse and Nuptse, it stood out as the dominating shape of a mighty trinity. " It stands infinitely high and distant against the blue-green sky," wrote Dittert. " In a supreme dynamic thrust, it is the climax and consummation of those waves of tumultuous earth that pour in from every horizon." [1] Realizing that its summit towered up to nearly 20,000 feet above where they then stood, the Swiss were suddenly filled with a feeling of humility mingled with awe. They ran over all the varieties of good luck they would need for victory : fine weather, good snow, absence of wind, acclimatization of the climbers, and skill in choosing the best route. Immediately they began to have misgivings. . . . But they quickly banished such depressing thoughts from their minds, knowing that the paramount need for success is faith.

They noted further that the South-east Ridge looked manageable, and with renewed hope they pushed on and arrived at Namche Bazar, the home of the great Sherpas. There Tenzing's mother lived, a little old woman of eighty with a wrinkled face tanned by the mountain air. She had not seen her son for twenty-five years, and came to pay him a visit, bringing presents of *chang* and a sack of potatoes, a most valuable item in this unproductive land.

[1] Dittert, *Avant-premières à l'Everest*, p. 48.

Namche Bazar is the last place of any size in the valley. It consists of some sixty squat, rectangular houses in tiers one above the other up the steep, scrubby slopes of the surrounding hills. With their white fronts and rows of black windows, they look like lined-up dominoes ready to be picked up by a player. On the green, as the sole touch of gaiety in this austere village, stood an impressive May-tree : a giant rhododendron with magnificent red flowers.

Here the houses were not built of *pisé*, or puddled clay, as in Tibet ; they had solid stone walls, and a rough shingle-board roof built over an inner one of bamboo matting. Their one storey was reached by a dingy wooden staircase, and there in the one living-room a fire burned all day and night, filling the place with smoke, as the hearth had no chimney.

The insides of some of these houses suggested that their owners were comfortably off. One got this impression from the carpets on which guests were invited to sit, from the delicate china cups in which they were offered tea, from the paraphernalia of worship placed before the gilt Buddha, and from the number of copper gourds ranged on the shelves.

A busy caravan traffic passes to and fro through the village in summertime, as Namche Bazar is on the route, via the Nangpa La pass (19,050 feet), to Tingri Dzong. From Tibet come salt, borax, and wool, while Nepal exports rice, sugar, and paper.

From Namche Bazar a short trek across increasingly austere country brought them to Thyangboche monastery (13,000 feet). This lamasery, like so many places where men dedicate themselves to a life of contemplation, is beautifully situated. The surrounding greenery of pine, birch, and juniper blends agreeably with the pale red temple and the white monastic houses. The trees sweep gently downhill, and the valley winds away up to the forbidding barrier of Lhotse and Nuptse, above which rears the sparkling summit of Everest.

The Genevese were received by the Lama, who showed them round the monastery and offered them Tibetan tea. Only Lambert emerged with credit from the latter ordeal ; he drained not only his own cup, but those of his companions, which they passed to him as discreetly as possible.

Above Thyangboche they entered the deep Imja Khola valley. Here and there houses in dry-stone walling were still to be seen, and low-walled enclosures in which long-tailed black yaks grazed in the thin pastures.

They climbed on into still more inhospitable regions. The grass gave out, and there remained only the great stony undulations

Crossing Nepal

of the moraines. They had reached the Khumbu glacier basin. On April 22, a little over three weeks after leaving Katmandu, they set up their base camp at 16,600 feet in a sheltered bowl near a frozen lake. The landscape was awe-inspiring : northward lay Pumori ; Nuptse and Lingtren rose on each side of the heavy, frozen stream of the Khumbu glacier ; and in the south the dark hollow of the Imja valley was dominated by the glittering mass of Ama Dablam.

There was straight away great activity at the Base Camp. While some went off to reconnoitre a possible site for Camp 1, others went to photograph the tracks of the Abominable Snowman which were reported in the vicinity. One group made topographical surveys, while still another prepared the distribution of stores to the various camps, which involved an enormous amount of work. The stores were divided into unit batches, which were subdivided into secondary units. Unit A had priority, including as it did among other things cooking-gear. Only when this had been transported to a camp could that camp be occupied. This organization of porter traffic required clockwork precision, since it was realized that the success of the expedition would largely depend on it.

The First Assault

In reality Camp 1 was to serve as Base Camp, and was set up on the Khumbu glacier at the foot of the ice-fall, on an islet of moraine débris (see map, p. 157). It was thickly surrounded by *nieve penitentes*,[1] as if they were inquisitive to discover how men live. Their presence made the site feel like the North Pole ; and yet shortly afterwards members coming down from the higher camps found here a positively Mediterranean haven of warmth.

At this stage Dittert assumed the leadership of the expedition, and took to using military terms like ' attack,' ' reconnaissance,' ' fall back,' and ' assault.' He resolutely tackled the difficult problems of food-supplies and transport of stores. One of his complaints was against the low tents in which, in order to write, one had to lie face downward supported on the elbows. Up till then he had been, like Shipton, a believer in light expeditions, but he changed his mind as it became evident that each camp must be equipped to become in its turn a base camp, and that in order to have four men, an assault party and a support party, at above 26,000 feet, three hundred men would have to be brought from Katmandu.

The Swiss were aware that they had two major obstacles to overcome before coming to grips with Everest proper : the ice-fall

[1] See above, p. 43.

I

.and the slope of the South Col. They felt particularly impatient to tackle those seracs which had earlier turned back Shipton and company.

While the establishment of Camp 1 was being completed a few of them went off on reconnaissance. Travelling up a sort of corridor flanked by walls of greenish ice, they attacked the ice-fall from the left. For six hours they wandered backward and forward in the maze in search of a way through in sixteen inches of powdery snow. It was obvious that danger lurked at every step, for all round them seracs were continually collapsing. After climbing

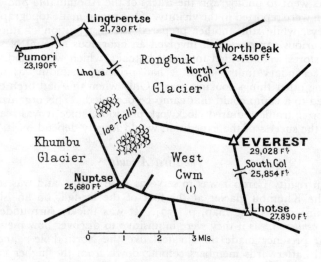

The Approach from the South

1200 feet they planted a flag as a landmark, and came down again.

The following day up they went again. Beyond the flag they began to wander about once more in search of a way on the right sheltered from the avalanches which fall from the West Ridge of Everest, but they failed to find a route towards the centre of the glacier.

On the third day they returned to the fray and set up Camp 2 half-way up the ice-fall on a cube of ice surrounded by crevasses. The site was far from safe, and one morning they awoke to find a fresh crack opened up between the tents !

Daily they set out, and daily they were thrown back on to the left by the way the crevasses ran. In despair they tried the avalanche corridor running close under the West Ridge. It was, of course, fully in Everest's firing-line, but as it was the only way they decided to make the best of a bad job and risk it.

The ' suicide run,' as they called it, did give them quite a few frights. One day Dittert's heart was in his mouth as he heard an avalanche roaring down just after his friends had set out. He hardly dared to breathe until he picked up Lambert's voice on his radio receiver saying, " Oui, on a vu le Nègre ! "—a Swiss climber's expression meaning, " We nearly had it that time ! " The avalanche had fallen half a minute ahead of the party.

Gaining ground steadily, they eventually reached the gateway to the West Cwm. Here they were halted by an enormous crevasse —no doubt the one which held up Shipton, for it barred the whole basin. They followed it, looking for a likely crossing-place, but with no luck. Finally they returned to the point where the chasm was no more than a few yards wide. There, wedged across, forty-five feet down, was an ice-block from which it might be possible to reach the other side.

Asper, the acrobat of the party, was lowered at the end of a rope into the abyss, which he crossed, stepping as lightly as possible (for one can never be sure of the strength of the blocks, which may or may not be firmly wedged), but when he sought a foothold on the opposite wall he could see that it was overhanging above him, so further effort was useless. He was pulled up, and soon the party was once more on the beat along the crevasse ; unfortunately, no other way of crossing showed up, so they turned back.

The following day they steadfastly returned to the same spot, where Asper was again roped down into the crack. Nineteen feet down he braced himself against the wall and pushed himself with all his might. He touched the block with his foot but then swung back and bumped against the wall of ice. A second attempt was no more successful, and so he gave up this " method of making the meat tender," [1] which proved far too painful.

He then tried another way. His companions lowered him into the blue abyss, this time to a depth of sixty feet, on to a bridge of fallen blocks. From that point he cut a ' chimney ' upward, and eventually managed to plant his axe in that all-important ice-block, where he stopped to recover strength. But his labours were not at an end ; he still had to scale a difficult cleft which brought him out on the far side, where he emerged in a state of exhaustion. " My arms and legs were like wet rags," he said. " I hadn't the strength even to blow my nose." [2]

When he had recovered his breath he fastened the rope round

[1] Dittert, *op. cit.*, p. 89.   [2] *Ibid.*, p. 90.

his ice-axe, wedged himself into a hole, and Flory then swarmed across. Thereupon the two men made a bridge of four ropes, secured firmly to wooden struts, which they bound together with rope-rings. Piling snow on to this anchorage, they set about hardening it by first subjecting it to an entirely unsophisticated process of wetting, so that it would set into a hard cement.

At first the Sherpas showed a distinct dislike for the rope manœuvre, but after a little while they grew quite used to it, and found the hauling over of the loads highly entertaining. It is true that nothing could have looked so ungainly as a pack swinging in this way over a void.

Following this spectacular piece of mountaineering Camp 3 was established at the entry into the West Cwm, towards the middle of the glacier (see map opposite). The first load to arrive was greeted with a cheer !

The expedition could now see right along the West Cwm as it lay between the blue-green walls of Nuptse and the icy spurs of Everest, and rose gently to the base of Lhotse.

Their ardour redoubled at the thought of being henceforth on virgin terrain. Throughout the approach trek they had been unable to dispel a certain amount of anxiety : " Shall I stick it out ? How high shall I get ? " each member continually asked himself ; and every man was so desperately anxious to be found fit for the last lap that if he took his pulse and it was found to be 80 he was sorely tempted to say that it was only 63.

They were over the first hurdle, and now contemplated the second : the South Col slope barring the far end of the Cwm. The upper part was divided by a rocky spur. Two ascent routes were possible here : one up the spur, the other in the right-hand couloir under the vertical face of Lhotse. The latter slope was long and uniformly steep, and thus subject to avalanches ; moreover no level portion offered a likely camp site on it, as far as could be seen. And finally, bearing in mind that it rose over 3000 feet, could one ask the porters to climb it with their loads at one stretch ?

With Camp 4 set up at the end of the Cwm and Camp 5 beneath the face of Lhotse, the party set out, looking like smugglers from the North Pole, with fur caps, down jackets, Lapp boots, three weeks' growth of beard, lips white with ointment, and wearing great goggles ! They all had ' bellows to mend,' having made the discovery, alas ! that their brand of oxygen apparatus was unusable on the move. Those closed-circuit sets made breathing too much of a toil, and could be used only during halts. What a bitter disappointment for them !

Attempts were repeatedly made over several days, first up, then back, then up again. They climbed part of the rocky rib which they christened the Éperon des Genevois, or Geneva Spur,

EVEREST 29,028 Ft
SOUTH SUMMIT 28,720 Ft
LHOTSE 27,890 Ft
28,215 Ft
CAMP7 27,550 Ft
South Col
CAMP 6 25,854 Ft
VIII
Geneva
Spur
VI
North
Col
NUPTSE 25,680 Ft
CAMP 5
22,630 Ft
CAMP 4
21,150 Ft
LHO LA
ROPE BRIDGE
CAMP 3 19,360 Ft
CAMP 2
19,030 Ft
CAMP 1
17,220 Ft
BASE CAMP 16,560 Ft

Route taken by the Swiss Expedition
Spring route : continuous line.
Autumn route : broken line.

and occasionally tried to get away from it on to the snowy slope at the side for the sake of making more speed, but every time they were thrown back towards the rocks by the glassy ice. They tried also to travel up the couloir of Lhotse, but found ice there too.

All of which forced them to the conclusion that the only practicable route was that of the rocky Spur.

They took the plunge, resolved to reach the South Col in one go, but as luck would have it the sky, which that morning had been clear, became slightly overcast, and clouds began to come down. One by one Everest, Lhotse, Nuptse, and the South Col were blotted out, and resignedly the climbers came back down, only to find Camp 5 in magnificent sunlight at noon, which drew from Dittert the remark " It's never as fine as when you've packed up ! "

A fresh attempt was made the next day. Everest was without its ' plume,' and this time the sky remained clear. Nevertheless, the party did not get as far as was expected. After ten hours of exhausting climbing, they had to face the facts—they were not going to reach the col before nightfall, so they excavated two platforms with their ice-axes and pitched two tents. They all crawled in, still roped and wearing crampons. They huddled close to each other to keep warm, for there was too little room to use sleeping-bags. Lambert drove his axe deep into the snowy slope, and made his rope fast to it.

In the morning, after a shocking night, Tenzing crept into the tent with a " Fine day, sahibs ! " and brought hot chocolate. Heaven knows how he had managed to heat it up ! Then, as the weather was indeed fine, they continued their slow and laborious ascent.

At last, at ten o'clock, the hump of ice overlooking the South Col was reached, at a height of 26,000 feet. For many it was a high-altitude ' baptism ' ; for some of the Sherpas it was the kind of exploit that had already earned them the right to the honoured title of ' Tigers.'

The final lap to the South Col is a descent. Before embarking on it the Swiss party glanced up at Everest, which now revealed itself for what it was, without any deceptive effects of foreshortening through being seen from below : sharp, sinewy, and powerful, with a lofty, imposing ridge. Even so, the white point stabbing upward into the blue sky is not the true summit, but only the south summit, with the highest point concealed behind it. They wondered what obstacles still stood between it and them.

But this was no time for idle speculation ; the camp had to be set up.

The South Col, like the North, is one of the least hospitable places on earth. It is a broad threshold to the mountain, over which there blows unremittingly a fearful, wild, icy wind, which scours the snow away down to the bare boulders. Pitching the tents was a terrible job. They flapped wildly as the wind tore at them, and only by crawling on all fours could the party hold their ground and get the tents up.

But windy nights at 26,000 feet are anything but restful, and

A.J.V.

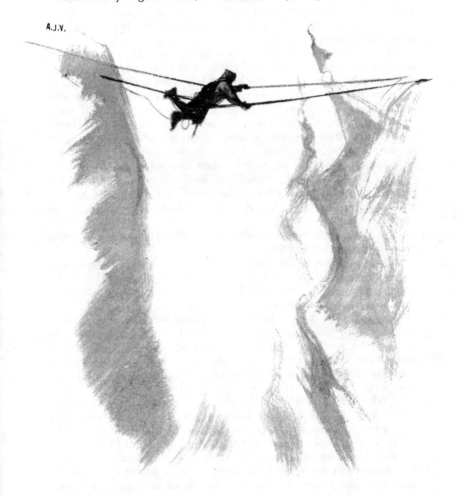

they wear down the energy of the fittest. The following morning the Sherpas, with the exception of Tenzing, were obviously at the end of their tether, and had to be sent back to Camp 5. The four remaining men, Lambert, Aubert, Flory, and Tenzing, looked inquiringly at each other. How would they manage to take up on to the South-east Ridge all the equipment necessary for setting up Camp 7 ?

They decided, at all events, to see what could be done, and, setting off on two ropes, with a tent and a small quantity of food, they crossed the flat part of the Col and made for the base of the South-east Ridge.

They tried to turn the first rock-step by way of the eastern slope, but then ran up against ground rising at sixty degrees, and soaring skyward. So they turned back and traversed round the base of the spur into a couloir. Here the climbing was steep but otherwise not difficult, and they rose steadily up through snow and rock, cutting their way, and taking frequent turns at leading. From time to time they stopped to drink in oxygen as they might have sipped a fine liqueur. Then off they started again.

Lambert and Tenzing were the first to reach a shoulder of the Ridge. Then Tenzing, breathless and hoarse, pointed to the summit and said twice over to Lambert in English, " You . . . and me. To-morrow ! " And twice Lambert replied, " No good ! " [1]

Yet there they were clumsily and fumblingly putting up their tent and preparing to camp.

There was room for two only, so when Flory arrived with Aubert he said to the others, " You two stay, and we'll wait for you at the col." They halted, and the three friends embraced each other before separating.

So, at 27,550 feet, Camp 7 was pitched—more of a bivouac than a camp, indeed, for the two occupants had not foreseen the necessity of spending a night in the tent, and had brought no mattress or sleeping-bag, or Primus. They had a frightful night, " one of those nights that make eternal hell-fire seem a pleasant prospect," [2] as Lambert put it.

Under the onslaughts of the vicious, icy wind, the tent flapped like a Buddhist prayer-flag. Lambert's hands were so numb that he " gave up undressing even for the most legitimate of needs." [3]

Soon memories of those nights on the Aiguille du Diable began to return as he experienced again the effects of extreme cold, " that bunching-up of the whole body until it feels ready to split, the face that feels like stone, the muscles contracted and rigid as though anæsthetized." [4]

The two men huddled up together, shook and thumped one another in a kind of slow motion to keep awake, and maintain some semblance of circulation. Being desperately thirsty, they used

[1] Lambert, A l'assaut des ' quatre mille,' p. 190.
[2] Ibid., p. 223.   [3] Ibid., p. 221.   [4] Dittert, op. cit., p. 169.

At Camp 4, the West Cwm.   In the background, Pumori

an empty cheese-box in which to melt a little ice over a candle-flame.

The wind continued to pummel the tent, frenziedly trying to sweep such a ludicrously flimsy intruder from the upper slopes. Suppose it should succeed ! What a terrifying thought ! To bolster up his morale Lambert thought of his companions down there, ready to come to his aid, and of the chain of camps linking Tenzing and himself to the world of men. . . .

Time did not pass, it stood still, and Lambert later recalled how he had imagined himself toiling up to the summit, and the struggle it would be, and the agony he would have to endure. "And the fact is," he remarked, "that my imagination was not strong enough ! " [1]

At last came the moment they had ceased daring to hope for. The darkness gave way to a pale grey, and on the slowly lightening canvas behind him the bunched form of Tenzing began to show up. Dawn was breaking. But not an encouraging one, alas ! As soon as they opened the tent-flap they were met by gusts of wind which hurled stinging snow-flakes in their faces. They looked up at the sky, and saw that it was completely overcast ; in the west and south big black clouds enveloped the peaks. They wondered what to do, and waited a little while.

Since by six, however, the weather was as bad as ever, they set off towards the summit. Progress was terribly slow : " One step, three breaths, another step, three breaths . . . we dribbled into our oxygen masks." [2] A third step, three breaths. . . . They wanted to open their chests as they would have unbuttoned a tight coat.

Every twenty yards the one leading gave way to the other. When the slope steepened they crawled on all fours like dogs. Although they were dazed their mountaineering instinct warned them not to wander over to the right for fear of the cornices. On they climbed.

The wind tore at them harder still, and, while trails of mist fled by, the sleet whipped their faces. They pushed on, as the landscape below merged and sank away.

Lambert was now keeping an eye on Tenzing. The Sherpa looked his usual self, although every now and then he would rock on his feet as if trying to regain his balance. On they went.

Lambert began to talk to himself : " How are you getting on ? " he asked. " All right," was the reply. That deceptive feeling of well-being is the greatest of all dangers ! On the Aiguille du Diable

[1] Lambert, *op. cit.*, p. 224.
[2] *Ibid.*, p. 225.

too he had felt all right ! On they went, climbing higher and higher.

The weather had by now further deteriorated, and pellets of snow whipped harder and harder against their left cheeks. But the southern summit was so near. . . . Another rocky stretch, another snowy crest. . . . Just that little more. . . . But it was no use ! They stopped, and the decision was taken without a word being exchanged. One long look was enough. Each understood what was in the other's mind, and they began to descend.

They had no regrets, because they had no thoughts. Only a leaden body with the soul frozen out of it.

When they got back to their tent they found that the wind had already ripped two holes in it, so they abandoned it. Then, struggling against a terrible lethargy, and stopping as often as on the way up, they blundered down as best they could, slipping and stumbling, to the col.

There they faced a trifling climb up to the camp, yet felt they would never manage it. . . . They collapsed, and Flory and Aubert, who were coming up to meet them, dragged them, inert, to the tent, where they sank into a deep sleep.

The altitude they had reached on this side (28,215 feet) was about the same as the British had formerly touched on the North Face. But whereas the British had encountered technical difficulties on the last stage, the Swiss had nothing but clear terrain and easy climbing ahead of them. What had stopped them, then ? They had shown strength, skill, and pluck, but they had equally shown that these were not enough. They had been halted panting for breath on the threshold of the airless zone, that impenetrable magic circle. What was needed now ?

The Great Sphinx of these blue expanses of sky still held the answer to that riddle.

The Second Assault

At Camp 5 Dittert, Chevalley, Roch, Asper, and Hofstetter were anxiously awaiting news, and imagining all that could possibly have happened to Lambert and Tenzing in their attempt.

While Chevalley could not leave his binoculars alone, Dittert wrestled with his conscience and wondered whether he had done the right thing. Oughtn't he to have brought them back ? He kept looking up to the top of the spur where the climbers were due to appear, but could see nothing.

Finally, as the weather was fine, all decided to wait no longer but to move up to the South Col to make their own attempt. They

Everest from the South Col

climbed on to the spur, and at last, at about noon, spotted the others. They were coming down slowly. Tenzing could hardly walk, and had to be helped down ; the three Swiss appeared to have reached the limit of endurance. Dittert was horrified to see the ravages wrought on his companions by fatigue and exposure. Their faces were thin, deathly and drawn, their eyes and cheeks hollow. " A suffering beyond human scale and endurance had set its mark upon them." [1]

Lambert gave them some tips. " Be careful," he said, " to have the assault party supported at Camp 7 by comparatively fresh men. We found we couldn't get back up to the tent. But if the weather is fit, you'll manage it all right." [2]

The groups parted, and the ascent team toiled on its way. " We hoped each halt would bring real rest," said Dittert, " but each time we were disappointed. While we were at the halt we felt better, and our hearts slowed down. But in under half a minute after starting off again it was as if we had never stopped at all." [3]

Some of the Sherpas showed signs of giving up, but were urged to carry on. They were no longer the lively, nimble fellows who had bounded across the crevasses on the Khumbu, however. Now they were trailing slowly along.

Ten hours of stubborn, sustained exertion were needed to get them on to the crest overlooking the col. From there they could see two yellow dots three hundred feet lower down : the tents. They were being buffeted by a fierce wind, and the first Sherpas to arrive dived into them for shelter. Whereupon somebody shouted, " Come on there, there's a tent to put up ! " So, although frozen and exhausted, one or two of them, crouching double to avoid being blown over, struggled with flying canvas, while others cleaned out the tents left by the first party. Snow had blown into them, and indescribable chaos reigned inside : bacon, méta,[4] and Primus stove were all piled up in a jumbled heap.

The place was soon tidied up, for everybody had only one idea : to find escape and shelter from the piercing wind that blew mercilessly. " It was an absolutely steady wind that never eased or dropped for an instant. It seemed the very music of empty space." [5]

Following a rough night, the morning brought clear skies, but Everest was wearing its white plume. There was no point in setting out, for no man could ever breathe in that cloud of wind-driven

[1] *Avant-premières à l'Everest*, p. 178.   [2] *Ibid.*, p. 178.
[3] *Ibid.*, p. 178.   [4] A French form of solidified spirit.
[5] *Ibid.*, p. 180.

snow that flies like a flag from the summit on certain days—a kind of semaphore signal betokening high winds.

There was nothing to do but to wait, though at above 26,000 feet waiting is not the same thing as resting. At this height the human body is living on its reserves, which steadily give out. The process of attrition was all the more rapid this time as the men were confined to their tents, where, being reduced to inactivity, they ceased to react to anything, and yielded increasingly to lethargy and somnolence, and allowed their resistance to be sapped away.

The hours dragged by while the wind increased in force. From time to time one of them would inhale a little oxygen, another would go out to straighten a tent-peg tugged askew by the violent gusts, or tie up a broken rope. " Outside one got the strange impression of being the sole living creature in these wind-swept wastes of rocks and ice." [1]

So the day went by ; and the night, too. In the morning Roch, who was coughing continually, felt inclined to go down, and Hofstetter was disposed to follow suit. But after breathing a little oxygen he felt his courage renewed, and had no further wish to turn back. A discussion then followed, and at about noon the two men made up their minds. They spent two hours in preparation, and two more in filling their packs, fixing on their crampons, and roping up.

The others saw them off. It took them an hour to climb the slope leading to the Spur, over which they disappeared. Then suddenly they were seen returning. Hofstetter had thought it rash to launch into a long descent so late in the day. Their pace was too slow, and he was afraid of having to bivouac.

When they got back to the camp there was a row ; Roch was furious, and Hofstetter obstinate. Yet one should not be too hard in judging these men, whose physical and nervous resistance was at an end. Finally, somebody had the bright idea of giving the two antagonists oxygen to breathe, and peace was immediately restored.

Another night was spent on the South Col. The following morning, although the wind had eased and Everest had shed its plume, it was too late for an attempt. The effort needed merely to keep alive had drained away the last ounce of the party's strength, and they were now fit for nothing but getting down again.

It was then discovered that one of the Sherpas, Sarki, had not moved since he arrived. Rolled up in his down sleeping-bag, he was prostrate with mountain sickness. He had to be shaken violently to get him up, and make him put his boots on. He was

[1] Dittert, *op. cit.*, p. 183.

roped up and they set off, but before they had gone fifty feet he collapsed, vomiting. He was picked up and his pack taken away from him. Although he was helped along—for his condition was pitiful—he fell every few steps. Getting up to the ' shoulder ' was martyrdom for him, but fortunately the wind had dropped somewhat. If the storm had continued the Swiss would have been hard put to it to bring their sick porter down to safety. For there were times when each man was just strong enough to look after himself and nobody else. " You live the whole time on the edge of disaster in these altitudes," Dittert remarks.[1]

Before beginning the descent, the expedition cast a final glance at Everest. The little tent used by Lambert and Tenzing had disappeared from the South Ridge, and the mountain had returned to its pristine purity and solitude.

The descent had the psychological effect of making Sarki feel better, and he no longer sank down every few yards. Now he was able to go two whole rope-lengths ; then he would whistle, and the party would stop.

The hours went by, and the men dragged themselves along. Would Nuptse always be beneath them, and would the end of the Cwm never show up ? At about seven in the evening they were half-way down the Spur, at the food-dump they had placed there at the time of the first attack. Sarki was all in. Dittert and Chevalley would have liked to go down with the other roped parties, but the condition of the sick Sherpa would not permit it. There was nothing for it but to bivouac, which opened up all sorts of menacing prospects in view of the physical state of every single one of them ; but there was no alternative.

They all slid into their sleeping-bags and huddled up against each other, waiting for the hours to pass.

Sarki fell asleep immediately. Chevalley melted some snow in a water-bottle held over two burning candles. He had plenty of patience, because he had plenty of time. Dittert watched the stars coming out, one by one, huge and bright, while the mountains were enveloped in darkness.

When you stare for hours at those myriads of constellations, you slowly become aware of their imperceptible movement. As you finally observe the movement of a clock hand by concentrating your gaze upon it, so you can feel physically the motion of the celestial bodies and of the earth. At every nightly halt I waited impatiently for the moment when I would experience this motion of earth and heavens.[2]

[1] *Op. cit.*, p. 186.
[2] Dittert, *op. cit.*, p. 188.

The endless night wore slowly on. Up till then no one had thought it possible to sleep out of doors at 23,000 feet without coming to serious harm. But both Europeans and porters proved that the experience, far from being fatal, is quite endurable, since they all came through it with no very marked effects.

But they reached Camp 5 with a sudden sense of urgency, and their one thought was to flee down that accursed Cwm before the monsoon made it a death-trap, and to drop down once more into a blessed world of water, grass, flowers, and the sweet smell of naked earth !

As they drew towards the foot of the glacier Dittert said to himself, over and over again, " We have all come out of Khumbu unscathed, every one of us ! " And the thought brought him an unspeakable feeling of relief.

The Autumn Expedition

> Le vent qui vient à travers la montagne
> Me rendra fou !
> VICTOR HUGO

After the exertions and hardships of their two May attempts, the Swiss thought they had had enough of Everest for a time. But no sooner were they back in Geneva than their thoughts wandered towards the Himalayas once again. Of such stuff are mountaineers made ; they have high ideals and short memories. Their recollections are quickly sifted to leave only rousing thoughts, the rest sinking into oblivion. There is the classical example of the climber who, sweating and panting on a moraine, earnestly told himself that the following year he would go to the seaside. Yet the following year found him sweating and panting on the same moraine.

Then the ex-members recalled having heard some Himalayan experts maintaining that autumn should be a more favourable time than spring for the ascent of Everest. For then an expedition would not be dogged by constant fear of the monsoon ; that would be over, and they would enjoy the long periods of settled weather common in the later season. Tilman's party, too, had considered this course, without pursuing it any further, but that was because they were concerned with the North Face, which gets no sun from autumn onward. On the South Face the position regarding sunlight is different, and appeared sufficiently encouraging to justify an attempt on that side.

They recalled, moreover, that the Nepalese Government authorization was valid only for a year, that in 1953 the British would be on their way to Everest, and in 1954 the French. So, even if neither of these should succeed—and it would be unsafe to assume that neither would—the next Swiss attempt would not be due for three years.

So they decided to take the bull by the horns, and began to organize an autumn expedition. The team was to comprise three ' old hands ' : Dr Chevalley, who was to have charge, Lambert, and Dyrenfurth ; and four ' new boys ' : Spöhel, Reiss, Groos, and Busio.

Making use of the experience gained, the period needed for getting the equipment together was cut down to a month. Yet much more equipment would be needed than by the previous expedition. Because they foresaw that it was going to be wickedly cold, they made provision for generous reserves of clothing, sleeping-gear, etc., so that the expedition carried not five tons of stores, as before, but seven and a half.

They left Katmandu on September 11, and on the very earliest stages of the journey suffered through bad weather. Every after-noon, and often enough throughout the night too, there was either drizzle or steady light rain or downpours. They could not dry their clothes, particularly their boots, which remained soaked, and could not be greased. They often sank ankle-deep in mud, and at night turned in to sodden, muddy tents, which smelt musty and leaked, for they had shrunk, and the walls no longer met.

The rivers were swollen, and frequently had to be waded through hip-deep, because the bridges had been swept away.

In the valleys, where the dampness lingered, they were attacked by leeches, some of which were so tiny that they got through the eyes of their climbing-boots and ensconced themselves in their woollen stockings.

When, already soaked to the skin, they climbed on to higher ground, and found that there the rain turned to snow, they began to shiver. One day, as they approached a col above 13,000 feet, Chevalley discovered a porter standing under a block. The poor fellow's teeth were chattering, and he was shivering in every limb. His face was ashen, and his lips blue, and he was staring straight ahead, quite paralysed with cold. Chevalley gave him a good massage, and then transferred to the man his own woollen shirt, pullover, hood, and canvas dungarees.

Unfortunately, not all the porters met their Good Samaritans in this way. Among those who were later in distress among the snows, two died of exposure.

Chevalley himself fell ill. Through pushing on, wearing only a light shirt and a blanket over his shoulders, he caught a chill,

and became feverish. And as if that were not enough, a leech-bite
in his ankle became inflamed, and he began to limp.

Not before arrival at Namche Bazar on September 28 did the
expedition strike good weather. There, for the first time since
Katmandu, the tents could be pitched on dry ground.

From there 325 men, a real invasion army, travelled up the
Khumbu valley, and very soon the Base Camp and Camp 1 were
set up. It was colder than it had been in the spring, the night
temperature falling as low as 12° (F.).

After so much trouble and discomfort, one pleasant surprise
was in store : conditions on the ice-fall were better than they had
been the previous time. The thaw had packed it down and fused
the blocks together, so that there were fewer holes, seracs, and
'chimneys.' It would be possible to find a safer way through
towards the centre.

However, the expedition was not in the best of health : sickness,
in the form of sore throats, colds, bronchitis, neuritis, pain in
breathing, and blood-poisoning, was common, and reduced the
potential energy of the party.

One of the porters was suffering from a huge abscess which
puffed out his neck like a tumour. His condition steadily deteriorated, until Chevalley was obliged to operate to save the man's
life. In an operating theatre improvised in the mess-tent, and
upon four large boxes, the operation was performed. Having
administered an anæsthetic, the doctor made a deep incision in the
neck, from which nearly a pint of revolting pus oozed out. The
Sherpas helping stared in horrified amazement ! But the patient
was saved !

Camps 2, 3, 4, and 5 were established, and immediately the
wind rose, making the period spent in the Cwm one of real hardship.
It roared on the heights and down the glacier, sweeping up the
snow and hurling it in the faces of the party and over the camp.
When it was at its most violent there was nothing for it but to
barricade themselves in and wait, the sole entertainment being
the coming and going of the loyal Sherpas who brought the meals,
collected up cups and plates, and took care after every visit to
close up the tent again tightly.

Lambert, Gross, and Tenzing launched the attack on the South
Col slope, following their spring route, and rising up to the Geneva
Spur. But they were hindered in their ascent by bare ice. They
cut steps and placed a fixed rope, but in two days they had climbed
only half-way to the food-dump, whereas in the spring they had
reached it at a single stretch.

During one of these assaults an accident occurred. While

the roped parties were spaced out above each other, a block of ice fell from the seracs high up on the Lhotse glacier. As they heard it tearing down they hunched their shoulders, crouched down, and hung on to the slope as best they could, gripping their ice-axes or the continuous rope. When the avalanche had passed by it was seen that a Sherpa was hanging head downward on the rope. He was held, groaning, by his companions, who managed to pull him up on to his feet. The poor fellow had been hit in the face ; his goggles were broken, and his face covered with blood, and it was a hard job getting him down below the bergschrund.[1] There, while Chevalley was examining his injuries, a cry was heard, and three other Sherpas, who had lost their footing on the slope, slid six hundred feet at an alarming speed, but without doing themselves much harm. Poor Mingma Norbu, however, died of his injuries, for not only had the ice-block hit his head, it had also broken several ribs, causing a serious perforation of the lung.

After this sad episode, the Swiss decided to abandon the Spur route, and turned towards the Lhotse glacier, where, although the slope was steep, there were easy stretches, and even level ones suitable for those indispensable camps. There remained one big question-mark : the traverse which would have to be made higher up to rejoin the top of the Spur. All would be well if it were still in the same condition as in the spring, when Chevalley had reconnoitred it

Laboriously weaving back and forth, up and down, cutting steps and fixing continuous ropes, Lambert and Tenzing managed to set up Camps 6 and 7 on the Lhotse glacier (see map, p. 157).

It was killing work, as daily the cold grew more intense, and the hours of sunshine fewer, and the wind never eased. At Camp 4 the sun had gone by one o'clock in the afternoon, at Camp 5 the temperature at three o'clock was −4° (F.), and at Camp 7 the night temperature was −22° (F.).

The wind was deafening. It bowled over casks, blew boxes all over the place, kept the men awake, and got really on their nerves.

One night Chevalley was awakened by a loud crack. The metal pole of his tent had snapped, and the canvas was immediately clapped over him. He could feel the pressure of the wind through it, and struggled vainly with both hands to free himself. Then he shouted, but nobody heard. So he stayed, imprisoned thus, for several agonizing hours. . . . .

Dyrenfurth also complained of one particularly bad night.

[1] The crevasse separating a glacier or snow-field from a steep, rocky slope.

" I cannot recall any time in my life when I was so near to madness,"
he said.

> From time to time I would light a lamp, and the fact of seeing its bright
> beam thrown on to the frantic wall of the tent seemed to restore some
> semblance of reality. But when I shone the light on to Gabriel's face,
> I could detect something suggestive of madness in his expression, too,
> the look of a wounded or dying animal. [1]

The party's morale was beginning to suffer badly. Undermined
by sleeplessness, and the struggle against wind and intense cold,
the Swiss were in anxious mood, and inclined to pessimism. It
was indeed high time for them to make an assault. There was, of
course, no pressure from an approaching monsoon this trip, and,
despite the wind, the weather remained fine. What did threaten
was grave physical and moral deterioration among the team,
which was going on apace as the cold intensified.

On November 19 Lambert and Tenzing attacked the South
Col slope with porters in clear weather. The much-feared traverse
passed without incident, through good snow, and the party was
on the col in the afternoon. Immediately they were harried by
the wind, and faced a frightful task in pitching their tents. The
moment the first two were up the Sherpas dived into them for
shelter, and there was no getting them out ! The night was un-
endurable, with a temperature of −40° F. Lambert lit two candles
in an attempt to warm his fingers.

The following day the hurricane was blowing even more
fiercely, and, as the sun would not reach the col before ten o'clock,
they delayed their departure, and did not leave until 11.30. They
had intended to set up a Camp 9 on the South-east Ridge, but
could not even set foot on Everest.

As they crossed the wide threshold formed by the col they felt
a paralysing coldness taking a grip on them. Their noses, fingers,
and ears were freezing. They travelled up the slope leading to
the Ridge, and there, flattening themselves against a wall of snow,
they noticed the remains of an eagle. " Well, and you've found
your master, too ! " Lambert remarked.

At 26,575 feet they had reached their limit, and they stopped.
. . . And then the rush back began ! They threw off their loads
and at the col discarded part of their equipment. At Camp 7 they
left food, canisters of oxygen, and half a mile of fixed rope.

All Everest steamed in icy fury ; the Cwm was a white hell of
swirling snow, the tents cracked and ripped, everything flew in
all directions in a frightful chaos. Tenzing had to shout to urge

---

[1] Dittert, *op. cit.*, p. 268.

on the Sherpas, for they were being buffeted about by the wind, and frequently blown over.

Only on emerging from the Khumbu ice-fall did they find calm air in which they could relax. While they were devouring chops, potatoes, liver, and beans, the Great Peak continued to roar its fury to the four corners of the world.

How it shrieked and bellowed ! Had it by chance some presentiment that the day of reckoning was at hand ?

A.J.V.

A.J.V.

CHAPTER XVI

THE BRITISH EXPEDITION OF 1953

MALLORY spoke the truth when he declared that climbers must have ' good fortune ' [1] above all things if they are to win through.

Fate decreed this good fortune for the British expedition in 1953. Looking at the venture as a whole, one is surprised how far they were favoured. A happy combination of circumstances gave them fine weather at the very moment when their fittest and best equipped pair were ready for the attack on the last lap.

They were, of course, worried by frequent snow-storms while

[1] Howard-Bury, *Mount Everest: The Reconnaissance, 1921*, p. 279.

negotiating the Khumbu ice-fall and the Lhotse glacier, but they do not seem to have had to put up with those frightful hurricanes which had earlier been such an ordeal for the pioneers of the North Face, and which had driven back the Swiss in 1952. The photographs furnish proof of this ; for while the Swiss are never to be seen moving about in the West Cwm unless muffled up to the eyes, the British are shown without gloves, and often enough in shirtsleeves.

Much of the talk of the luck of the British is perhaps attributable to the fact that they were both highly versatile and competent. For are not luck and ability closely related, and does not one often enough depend on the other ? When he heard anybody's ability being praised, Cardinal Mazarin always used to ask, " Is he lucky ? "

The first merit of the British was in finding, in the person of Lieutenant-Colonel (now Brigadier Sir John) Hunt, a real leader. A Regular Army officer who had served in India, Hunt had wide experience of the Himalayas and of the inhabitants of the surrounding lands. During various missions he had lived the life of the natives, and he spoke Bengali and Urdu fluently. As a mountaineer, too, he had given ample proof of his skill, rounding off ten seasons of Alpine climbing with two expeditions to the Karakoram range and the Kanchenjunga massif respectively. And finally, in addition to organizing ability, he could command respect through that rare gift which is the essence of leadership : natural authority. While the Swiss were a team of friends, acting in consultation, and on a basis of absolute equality, to decide questions affecting the common interest, it appears that Hunt was always in command, assigning tasks and taking decisions which it never occurred to anyone to question, for they always seemed judicious and well thought out.

He admits that, on receiving from the Himalayan Committee a telegraphed invitation to take charge of the 1953 expedition, he was torn between equally strong feelings of enthusiasm and apprehension. To the mountaineer it was a crowning honour, to the man a heavy burden of responsibility.

He immediately set to work, however, and succeeded in enlisting co-operation. He distributed the work among the members of the expedition to such effect that, three months before their departure, they all found themselves drawn into a busy organization, each with his allotted task.

When it came to choosing the party Hunt was in a quandary. There were many candidates whose qualities justified their. inclusion. Four factors appeared paramount : age, experience, character, and constitution. Hunt wanted men between twenty-five and forty, rightly estimating that between those ages a man possesses the maximum stamina. The question of ideal physique for Himalayan climbing had often been discussed. Were long legs or sturdy build the greater asset ? The question of height, as a matter of fact, is irrelevant. The general physical make-up is the thing, the relation between weight and strength, and the fitness of the system to stand up to hardship.

Hunt was, moreover, looking for men with the will to win, but not averse to assuming a secondary rôle if, in the course of the attack, circumstances should demand it. And he found them.

Some virtually picked themselves ; these were the ones who had accompanied Shipton in 1951 on the first reconnaissance of the Khumbu ice-fall, and those who, also with Shipton, had been members of the training expedition to Cho Oyu in 1952. These included Hillary, Bourdillon, Evans, Gregory, and Dr Ward.

At Thyangboche, after his Everest attempt, Dittert had met Hillary on his way from Cho Oyu, and had complained of the difficulty that all the Swiss had experienced in getting time off from their various occupations for the expedition. Hillary's reply had been that " for him it was no problem, because in New Zealand he had thousands of workers so conscientious that they required no particular supervision and worked perfectly well in his absence." Seeing Dittert's astonishment, he had added with a smile, " I have lots of bees who can manage very well without me for a few months." [1]

The party included another New Zealander, Lowe. Like Hillary he had gained his mountaineering experience among the snowy peaks of his native isles in the Pacific, which reach their highest point in Mount Cook (12,350 feet). Both had, moreover, been trained to contend with wind and snow, for, according to Irving, in New Zealand " you can reckon on no more than a day and a quarter of fine weather in a week." [2] But perhaps he was exaggerating.

To complete the party there were Wylie (an officer from a Gurkha regiment), Noyce, Pugh (physiologist), Westmacott, Band, and Stobart (camera-man). This made thirteen members, a fact which Hunt took care not to advertise, because it might be regarded as unlucky. He was therefore greatly relieved when Tenzing agreed to come in and make one more. It should, incidentally, be understood that, although theoretically Tenzing was engaged to lead the Sherpas, he was from the start regarded by the British as a full member of the climbing party.

[1] Dittert, op. cit., p. 198.
[2] R. L. G. Irving, Ten Great Mountains (Dent, 1940).

Tenzing had been heart-broken on receiving, *via* the Darjeeling office, Major Wylie's invitation, because he was still making only slow progress towards recovery from an attack of malaria, contracted during the return from the Swiss autumn expedition—an illness which had kept him in hospital for a long time. But so strong was the little fellow's mountaineering fever that it ousted the other. Wylie's offer acted as a stimulant, and he was on his feet, and in next to no time running up and down mountains to recover his strength, which he succeeded in doing beyond all expectation.

For their reappearance on the Everest scene the British insisted on the most efficient and up-to-date equipment. This time it was understood that everything was to be thrown into the drive for victory, and to that end suggestions were asked for from inventors.

One inventor suggested a powerful catapult capable of hurling a grappling-iron from the South Col to the summit. The rope was to be coated with phosphorescent paint to enable the climbers to go on hauling themselves up even after nightfall.

In the gardens of the Royal Geographical Society a modest version of this contraption was tried out. When the strong elastic was released the iron shot straight up on the end of its nylon rope and over the garden wall. There was great fear that it might have transfixed a passer-by or the hood of a car, but fortunately it had stuck in a tree.

Another inventor had the idea of setting up a great oxygen reservoir in the West Cwm, from which a pipe-line would run up the route of the climb, with taps on it to enable the party to refresh themselves periodically with ' swigs ' of the gas.

Somebody suggested attaching ' hydrogen wings ' to the climbers' shoulders to reduce their weight—without entirely eliminating it, of course, for it would be necessary to clear themselves of any accusation of having flown up Everest ! But they could not quite see themselves floating up the ridge on tiptoes. Besides, when they found out what size such balloons would have to be they shuddered to think of the amount of surface they would offer to the wind.

Rather more serious was the suggestion that equipment might be parachuted on to the South Col; although there were fears that the wind, which never abated there, might make it impracticable.

Another possibility was a sledge to transport the loads into the West Cwm. But on the one hand the difficulty of getting up quantities of fuel for the winch-motor, and on the other hand the impossibility of finding any even stretch of ground for the sledge to run on, led to the abandonment of the project.

The Army had been asked to provide a small mortar for bringing down avalanches. The climbers were delighted at the prospect of using it—it made such a lovely bang ! But as things turned out it was left at Base Camp, and only used after the party had come down again, to celebrate the victory !

Above all else, credit must go to Hunt for grasping the importance of the oxygen question. Valuable lessons were to be learnt from the experiences of the Swiss expedition in this connexion. Lambert and Tenzing had been halted on the South-east Ridge, not by bad weather, but by suffocation. If that mountaineering phenomenon the Swiss guide, and the toughest of tough Sherpas, had failed to climb Everest on the strength of their own lungs, then men would have to be provided with an extra lung. Dittert had said feelingly, " Oh, if one could only breathe oxygen while climbing, what a difference it would make." [1]

Hunt gave Bourdillon the job of putting the oxygen respirators in order, aided by Peter Lloyd, who during the 1938 expedition had studied the whole question thoroughly.

Experiments were carried out in the decompression chambers of the R.A.F., and during one of these Hunt, who was watching through a window, witnessed a disturbing sight. When the air-pressure had been reduced to resemble conditions at 29,000 feet one of the members of the expedition had his mask removed, whereupon through the effects of asphyxiation his tongue began to hang out of his mouth. The experiment clearly took no account of the progressive acclimatization which would result from gradually climbing to that altitude. That such acclimatization did, in fact, operate, and make results very different on the climb, was shown by the fact that Hillary removed his mask for a quarter of an hour on the summit, and felt nothing worse than slight difficulty in breathing. But how strange to think that the layer of humanly breathable air above our heads rises to no more than five and a half miles !

The expedition was to carry two types of oxygen set with open and closed circuits. The second guaranteed a supply of oxygen for a longer period than the first, which nevertheless gave greater relief, and allowed Hillary and Tenzing to reach the summit.

The question of boots and gloves was particularly important. In the past there had been only too many sad instances to prove that frost first attacks the extremities. Two types of boots were considered. The first, intended to be worn up to the West Cwm, was a comparatively close-fitting type ; the other, designed for higher altitudes, was very broad. It had a micro-cellular rubber sole,

[1] Dittert, *Avant-premiéres à l'Everest*, p. 183.

and was stuffed inside so as to insulate the inner two-fifths of an inch of thickness from the outer. And it was wonderfully light, being no more than two pounds in weight.

Three pairs of gloves were allowed to each climber : a silk one to be worn almost continually, one in down, and one in windproof cotton. The three pairs, worn on top of each other, were very flexible, and allowed freedom to wield an axe for cutting steps.

As they were now fitted up with clothing, the next job was to find them shelter. Tents were made with interior and exterior entrances (' sleeve entrances '). This innovation was designed to allow one tent to be joined to another, and would be particularly appreciated in high winds. And for the South-east Ridge ultra-light, miniature tents were made, weighing eight pounds each.

Then a type of double-thickness, air-filled mattress was produced. As each air-tube in the upper layer was placed between two in the lower (and vice versa), no cold air could blow through—a snag familiar to campers in high altitudes. Finally each man was provided with two down sleeping-bags.

The remaining problem was the all-important one of food, and it was decided that the expedition should live on Army rations.

Early in December 1952, when already a great deal of thought had gone into questions of equipment, Hunt and a few companions went to Switzerland to test everything, not wishing to leave anything to chance. He set up a camp on the Jungfraujoch at 11,500 feet. Conditions were perfect ; that is, they reproduced Himalayan conditions : a blizzard was blowing, and the temperature was −4° (F.). Every day they changed their tent, their sleeping-bag, and their clothing. Every day, in order to try out their eight types of footwear, they wore a different shoe on each foot. In this way they picked out the best articles, and were subsequently thankful for having done so.

In January 1953 Hunt set out, this time with his whole party, for the Welsh mountains, where the members got to know each other, and practised climbing with oxygen apparatus, which they found very awkward.

On several occasions Hunt had been in touch with the Swiss, who had generously furnished useful information. They had shown him their own equipment, and, in particular, they had told him of the places in the West Cwm where they had jettisoned food and oxygen reserves.

The colossal amount of equipment carried by the British expedition weighed seven and a half tons, and was divided into 443 loads. Everything was labelled and entered on a list, down to the last needle, the last box of matches, and stick of sealing-wax.

While all this was being loaded on to a train in Bombay, Wylie anxiously wondered how such a quantity of equipment and stores was going to be got up to the Khumbu glacier.

Blazing the Trail

The personnel and equipment of the expedition assembled at Katmandu in early March. The members converged in small groups from different corners of the earth, and Tenzing joined them from Darjeeling with eighteen hand-picked Sherpas.

When Wylie saw the varied assortment of would-be porters he refused to believe that they could be relied on to climb up the Khumbu ice-fall and on to the South Col. There were big ones, little ones, fat ones, thin ones. Some were in tattered clothes, and wore only Tibetan boots on their feet ; others were still wearing shorts, wind-cheaters, and felt hats—left-overs from previous expeditions. For it is customary in Himalayan mountaineering to allow the Sherpas to keep the kit issued to them. They often sell it, and in that way swell their profits.

There were Sherpa women among them, too. In the previous year the Swiss had taken on four of these women, and the experiment had been a great success, for they had pulled their weight admirably in load-carrying. Now they were there in greater numbers, either because they wanted to stay with a husband or sweetheart, or because the expedition offered a means of getting to some remote village. One might have expected their presence to be a source of jealousy and trouble among the porters, but that, oddly enough, was far from being the case. In fact, their cheerfulness and high spirits contributed to the happy atmosphere existing among the transport parties.

One of the key factors in the plan of attack, as Hunt had worked it out, was the training to be undergone by the party as a preliminary to tackling Everest. This part of the proceedings was carried out round about Thyangboche, where a provisional Base Camp was set up. For three whole weeks climbers and Sherpas were busy on the neighbouring mountains, among which they scaled six peaks of some 20,000 feet. This semi-holiday spell produced the hoped-for results, in raising the morale of the party to a high pitch of optimism, giving them a chance of acclimatizing themselves, of getting to know each other—for they frequently changed partners—and of training a few Sherpas in the use of the oxygen apparatus. During the approach trek the latter had often forced themselves to wear a disconnected mask simply in order to get used to it. These fellows took a childish delight in learning to breathe ' English air.' Wearing respirators, they would romp and lark about like puppies, and then go off on a trip, exclaiming on their return that with one of those things going up was as easy as coming down !

One day at Thyangboche camp Bourdillon made a horrifying discovery : fifteen of the sixty oxygen cylinders provided for the training climbs were empty ! The jolting during transit had caused them to leak. If the same thing had happened to the rest of the cylinders that would mean the erd of the expedition. For by the time a fresh supply had been sent for and got, the monsoon would be on them, and it would be too late. Hunt was appalled, and sent a message to the column which was still moving up with the bulk of the equipment. Happily the news was reassuring : the cylinders were in perfect order.

The British established their Base Camp on the site of the Swiss Camp 1—that is, under the Lho La (see map, p. 157). Immediately they attacked the first of the two great obstacles to be overcome before reaching the South Col : the ice-fall. They rejected from the start the route which had caused the Swiss such anxiety, and looked for a way through towards the middle ; but, according to the Sherpas, it was in a worse state than the year before. They certainly ran into considerable difficulty, and zig-zagged about ceaselessly, relieving each other when they became exhausted. No sooner had they reconnoitred the ground ahead and cut steps than they would have to repeat the process, for often enough a light fall of snow in the afternoon undid the work of the previous day.

Learning from the experience of the Swiss, they brought a quantity of stakes, rope, and metal ladders of various kinds, and wooden beams. They were thus able to place fixed ropes, throw bridges over crevasses, and generally open up the route. Noyce would chop away lustily at the base of a serac with his ice-axe, and then he and a squad of Sherpas would push a beam against it until it toppled over with a thunderous crash. The porters brought up tree-trunks and ladders which swayed precariously on their shoulders, and all the tiny black figures making their way up and down the glacier were as active as ants on the way to their ant-hill.

In order to find their way about more easily, the members of the party gave names to the different ways they had found through the ice-fall. The names tell their own tale : ' Hillary's Horror,' ' Mike's Horror,' ' Hell-fire Alley,' the ' Atomic Bomb Area,' and lastly ' The Nut-cracker,' where there was the risk of being crushed to death if the jaws of ice closed up

K*

Ice-falls on the Khumbu Glacier and a View of the West Cwm

For the glacier was changing shape rapidly. Every day new cracks opened, layers of ice fell down as if sliced off by an invisible knife, and seracs fell. The way had to be continually rerouted, the fixed ropes moved, and extensions added to the metal bridges which had become too short. Here and there little Swiss flags picked out a now impassable route. One was perched on top of a tower of blocks, another lay under a wall.

The constant movement of ice produced fearsome subterranean noises, caused by blocks breaking up, thumping down the walls of crevasses, and, after a moment's silence, sending up a deep boom which shook the ground. It was quite impossible to grow hardened to it. Then there was the crack of masses of ice splitting and throwing up walls overnight across the line of advance. Everywhere danger lurked. Nevertheless, surprising as it may seem, throughout the whole assault on the mountain the British were as fortunate as the Swiss had been in so far as no serious accident befell them on the ice-fall. What mishaps there were were of no significance.

After doing a first-class job of labouring and bridge-building for thirteen days without a stop, they noticed that gradually the slope was becoming less steep, the cracks narrower, and the glacier more even. They threw a final foot-bridge across, and on moving forward were overjoyed to see the length of the West Cwm before them. The ice-fall had been climbed !

They set to work forthwith transporting a quantity of equipment to the end of the Cwm for their Camp 4, which became the advanced Base Camp (see p. 157).

At Camp 3 they had already found a food-dump left by the Swiss, and they discovered another much bigger one at Camp 4. By digging in the snow the porters unearthed all manner of good things : chocolate, dried milk, biscuits, jam, Ryvita, bacon, cheese, etc. The party next examined the slopes of the South Col and Lhotse. They had heard so much about these places, and studied so many photographs of them, that they already had a familiar look. They had the choice of the spring and autumn Swiss routes. The Geneva Spur is undoubtedly the most direct way to the South Col, but it is steep, and in 1953 icy slopes barred the way to it. As the Lhotse face appeared more promising, they chose that, and followed in the footsteps of their predecessors, upward from camp to camp, finding much of their discarded material on the way.

Before launching the attack, Hunt allowed the climbers a few days' rest at Base Camp, which was much appreciated on account of a general atmosphere less harsh than in the higher camps. The members could relax, sleep, read, write, and listen to Radio Ceylon. On moonlight nights, as they left the mess-tent to go to bed, they could enjoy looking at the *nieve penitentes* glinting in the cool light, and at the metallic lustre of Pumori and Lingtren, while the ice-fall remained plunged in deep gloom. There was calm in the icy air, and absolute silence, intermittently broken by the murmured conversation of the Sherpas clustered round a lamp in their tent, or perhaps by the distant rumble of falling ice.

Hunt assembled the climbers in the mess-tent to put the plan of attack before them. It was a solemn moment, for it was felt that the rôles were to be cast, and every man wondered what his would turn out to be. They were half-lying on sleeping-bags, or sitting on wooden cases. Tenzing was standing near the door. No one spoke a word.

Then Hunt began to brief them. As soon as the South Col was reached, and Camp 8 established, four assault teams would set out from there at twenty-four-hour intervals. The first, comprising Evans and Bourdillon, would use closed-circuit equipment, and would make for the south summit—and higher, if possible. The second, composed of Hillary and Tenzing, would go and set up Camp 9 somewhere on the Ridge at about 28,000 feet, and from there make their attempt. They would use open-circuit oxygen sets. The other climbers would perform supporting tasks, such as establishing Camp 9 and transporting supplies.

For some time it had been evident to Hunt that Hillary and Tenzing worked perfectly together. They were of entirely different types. Hillary was tall and long-legged, and wore a striped cap that made him look like a fellah of the days of the Pharaohs. Tenzing was short and strongly-built. But they got along famously. Moreover, Hunt thought it only right to give Tenzing his chance to reach the summit ; for this was the Sherpa's sixth Everest expedition. Such unshakable grit deserved its reward.

The ascent of the Lhotse glacier placed a great strain on Hunt's nerves. Often as he trained his field-glasses on the climbers from the advanced Base Camp, their slowness reduced him to despair. This failure to travel at a faster pace was to be ascribed to the effects of altitude, to the snow-storms which frequently set them back, to the necessity of cutting steps over long stretches (in one climb Lowe was cutting for five hours out of seven), and to the need for placing fixed ropes stretching nearly 1000 feet.

The slope was steep, and cut up by cliffs with ledges running along beneath them. On one of these Camp 6 was pitched. It was reached with the aid of a rope fixed to stakes which had been driven into the wall of ice rising above it. Just round about the tent there was very little room to stand, no more, in fact, than the area of a table-top, and frequently falls of snow from above made it necessary to shovel a way in and out.

Lowe toiled and strove for ten days between Camps 6 and 7. Hunt sent him continual reinforcements to help, but there were sick men to be reckoned with, too. Band had fallen ill just as they were on the point of pushing on, and Evans had taken some drug and was unable to eat anything. Perhaps he had swallowed one of the pills which Dr Ward had handed round, cheerfully inviting them to " Try one ; they won't do you any good."

It really looked as though the party was going to find progress beyond Camp 7 out of the question. Every day they set out and got a little way up, only to be driven down again by deep snow, wind, and fatigue. Lowe was beginning to feel the altitude badly, and after taking a narcotic remained drugged for twenty-four hours. Noyce, who was with him on that day's effort, fell asleep as he was eating, with a sardine half hanging out of his mouth !

But Hunt was getting desperate. Time was passing, the way not yet opened to the Col, and the traverse not even begun ! In eleven days the men had climbed only half-way up the slope. This stage must be got over, particularly as the weather was beginning to improve.

So he took a momentous step. Although wishing to hold Hillary and Tenzing in reserve for the final assault, he decided to dispatch them as reinforcements. For after all, it was a case of taking things as they came. If there was to be such a thing at all as a final assault, the South Col would have to be reached first. The two men clearly realized that the assignment they were being given might well cost them the summit ; nevertheless, as the interests of all were at stake, they left without a moment's hesitation. Yet on the very morning they set out Hunt, whose eyes seldom left the serac concealing Camp 7, was taken aback at seeing two black dots appear on the snow. He grabbed his glasses. Yes, two men were attacking the slope ! They were moving up.

Noyce and a Sherpa, Annullu, were going bravely forward. They alternated in the lead, for the Sherpa travelled as well and as quickly as a Swiss guide, as Noyce observed. It was sometimes a job to find the best route, but in spite of twists and turns they managed to make progress. Several times they came upon Swiss ropes, which they did not dare to use, however, because they were no longer safe, their anchorages having worked loose. Then they encountered an ugly vaulted crevasse. To begin to get across they had first to forget what fear meant, then stand precariously on one overhanging lip, and stride across, gaining a foothold on the opposite lip, which was no less perilous.

Clutching his field-glasses to his eyes, Hunt saw the pair begin the traverse : the crucial part of the ascent. The great danger was that the snow might be treacherous. But it appeared to be causing no anxiety to the two men, who were going well and steadily.

This section, though technically not difficult, is quite spectacular. It cuts across the top of the slope which sweeps evenly down to the bottom of the Cwm like a length of white cloth. Lambert maintained that it would be possible to ski down it, though it rises at an angle of forty-five degrees. Down on the glacier Hunt walked some little way from the camp to get a better view of the movements of those small, dark-blue figures he was following with his field-glasses. He saw them coming up to the Geneva Spur, saw them silhouetted for an instant against the sky, and then disappear. With a sigh of relief he realized that at last the South Col route was opened.

But his worries were not at an end. He wondered why others had not managed to follow Noyce and Annullu, because there were plenty of Sherpas at Camp 7. Were they in such a bad way as all that ?

They were indeed suffering from extreme fatigue, headaches, and acute depression. But news that the Col had been reached had its effect, and when their own leader Tenzing arrived they took heart once more. Finally, a few tablets judiciously distributed round by Wylie added the finishing touch, and they were soon their old energetic selves again.

The following day Hunt picked out through his binoculars fourteen, fifteen . . . sixteen . . . seventeen black dots emerging from Camp 7 and making their way in succession up the slope. The transporting of the 650 lb. of supplies needed for the final assault had begun ! Hunt felt his heart warm towards those porters who, labouring against the effects of altitude and lack of sleep, and without the aid of oxygen masks, were manfully carrying up their loads. They had set out on no more sustenance than a cup of tea, and among them was a man of forty-eight, Dawa Thondup, a veteran who had been counted out by the doctor at Darjeeling, but whom Hunt had taken on as an old and trusted friend.

The following day, while Hillary and Tenzing were on their way down for a rest, other teams moved off, and Hunt too set out. When he descried Everest from the top of the Geneva Spur he was filled with dismay. A second mountain, massive, pointed, and powerful, rose from the South Col. He could hardly believe that after such exertions another problem of equal or greater magnitude still remained, and he was both alarmed and incensed at the thought.

" On the South Col death is in the air," Roch had told the British, but the latter had assumed that he was merely being colourful, dramatic, and generally Continental. But when they started to drop down into that vast funnel, with the wind howling through it as if it were a vacuum-cleaner, they began to wonder whether there might not be something in it. Their general impression was strengthened by the discovery of the skeletons of the Swiss tents. Only the supports were left, the wind having torn away all the canvas. Pegs and guy-ropes, still in place, preserved the three-dimensional, geometric outline of those once-time tents which now had the transparency of phantoms.

The establishment of the camp was a herculean struggle. The force of the wind was terrifying. It bowled about everything placed on the ground, tore the canvas out of porters' hands, wrapped the ropes round their legs, and tied the strings into endless knots. The Sherpas were staggering about like drunkards ; the Europeans were shouting at the tops of their voices, but their cries were inaudible five yards away. Hunt, who had removed his oxygen mask to give himself greater freedom of movement, tripped over a stone and fell full length, and it was five minutes before he could struggle to his feet again. Bourdillon also fell after taking off his mask, and was knocked almost unconscious for a moment. One Sherpa, completely distraught, took refuge in a half-pitched tent, and immediately the others handed him boulders and oxygen cylinders to stand on the canvas to prevent it from flying away.

All night the wind frantically assailed the camp, and the occupants found relief only by breathing oxygen. Fortunately, the unearthing of another Swiss dump had ensured an adequate reserve of the gas.

The First Assault

They were so worn out the following day that nobody in the camp stirred.

But on the morning of the 26th two roped pairs got ready to move off : Evans and Bourdillon, Hunt and the Sherpa Da Namgyal. While the first pair made the main attack the second would carry up the supplies needed to establish Camp 9.

It was bitingly cold in the tent. Bourdillon, who was struggling with a respirator, one of the valves of which was frozen, carelessly picked up a metal tool with his bare hand, only to drop it hurriedly, just as if he had touched a red-hot iron ; the tool fell with a shred of skin sticking to it.

Hunt and Da Namgyal were first off, carrying oxygen masks. With forty-five pounds on their backs they were well loaded, and they found it hard to get a footing as they crossed the Col. The wind-swept ice was so hard that the spikes of their crampons hardly made any impression on it. They were approaching the couloir used by the Swiss, and while they were toiling, cutting steps and stamping them flat, they were overtaken by Evans and Bourdillon, who were going well.

They let them pass, and laboured on, puffing and panting, until they finally reached the ridge where they found Lambert's tent with shreds of orange material fluttering from it in the wind. They halted there, feeling very tired. Hunt discovered later the reason for his own jaded feeling : the tube of his oxygen set was blocked, and for several hours he was thus deprived of the restorative effects of the gas. When they set off again their loads seemed heavier than ever, but they refused to give up.

However, at about 27,750 feet they could go no farther, so they stopped and dropped their loads. In the hollow of a rock they carefully laid out a tent, food, cylinders of oxygen, a candle, and a box of matches. Then they built a cairn of stones as a landmark, and came down.

They moved slowly, belaying each other alternately—a necessary precaution, for in the couloir Da Namgyal slipped and fell down the length of the rope. When they reached the slopes of the Col they were spotted by Hillary and Tenzing, who had just arrived, and who came up to meet them. Hunt felt his strength ebbing away as if the blood were flowing from his veins ; his knees gave way, and he collapsed. At his side Da Namgyal, too, sank to the ground.

While Tenzing gave them lemonade to drink, Hillary could see that they were not going to have the strength to move, and so went to fetch his oxygen mask from the camp. After inhaling a few lungfuls the two exhausted men could then be got to the haven of their tents.

On the ridge, however, Evans and Bourdillon kept up their fast rate of progress, and rose 1500 feet in two hours and a half. Their oxygen was working well, and they were in high spirits.

But gradually the conditions altered ; the weather deteriorated, clouds floated over the ridge, there was intermittent snow, and the wind was scouring the cornices. The thick powder-snow on the broken rocks made the utmost caution imperative. The two climbers were slowed down, but they still went on.

Soon, however, they were held up by a technical hitch. The

oxygen was getting low in the cylinders and they wondered whether to change them right away, at the risk of losing some of the gas, or wait. It was obvious that the higher they went the more difficult the operation would become, so they decided to do it then, but it was a tricky business, and valuable time slipped by before they were on their way once more.

They reached the foot of the long slope running up to the South Summit, and found that the snow on it could not be trusted. It consisted of a thick layer of crust over thick powder. If the crust gave there would be an avalanche falling 10,000 feet on to the Kangshung glacier !

Rocks on the left were a heartening sight under these circumstances. Moving with the utmost care, they risked a traverse, and when they felt their feet on firm ground again they heaved a great sigh of relief. Here the rocks are snow-covered, but their stratification runs the opposite way to that on the North Face, and at least they offer a firm foothold.

They climbed on, and at one o'clock were on the South Summit. Straight away they looked for that ridge never hitherto seen by mortal man, the ridge which for so many years had eluded Everest climbers : the final ridge ! It was itself free of cloud, but the clouds hovering round it somehow made it even more menacing in appearance. It looked narrow, and there were cornices edging it and masses of overhanging snow. The climbers were faced with the difficult decision whether or not to attack it forthwith, this being their only chance of the summit.

They thought it over : reckoning three hours to go up and two to come down, they would not be back on the South Summit until six, when their oxygen reserve would be used up, and they would still have to face a descent of 3000 feet to the South Col.

No, they thought, it would be madness. Wisely they turned back, without any regrets, for they had had a full day, having carried out their mission and climbed higher than any man alive or dead, reaching 28,750 feet.

The descent was a nightmare. Being no longer buoyed up by the will to conquer, they were all the more conscious of their fatigue. To save time, they cut straight down the perilous slope, sinking deep into the snow at every step, too weary to give a thought to the risks this course involved. They had only one thought : to get down !

Lower down their oxygen equipment gave them further trouble. They found it necessary to transform the sets into open-circuit types, then back to closed-circuit. Down the ridge they were constantly stumbling, through having partially lost control of their

legs. They fell over eight or ten times, and although Evans was
a good mountaineer he could not save himself on one occasion from
slipping, and crashing down on to Bourdillon, whom he also sent
flying. Both men slid down until Bourdillon, with a supreme
effort, twisted over face downward and drove his axe into the snow.

When he rose again he could see Evans lower down, and felt
envious of him, because his fall had taken him a good way down
that accursed slope !

Slowly they tramped back to camp, looking like divers rather
than climbers, or like men from another planet, with their bulging
kit, their unwieldy oxygen apparatus, and their masks covered with
thick frost. They were in a state of utter exhaustion.

From the South Col their companions had anxiously followed
their progress all day. Often they had been hidden by cloud, but

frequent rifts had kept them regularly in view. At about one o'clock Lowe had spotted them on the slope to the South Summit, looking like insects on a wall. Then they had climbed and passed out of sight, whereupon Lowe had poked his head into Hunt's tent and shouted, " They've got there ! My God ! They've got there ! " and every one had grown very excited. Not least the Sherpas, for they thought the white cone was the summit. They had leapt and yelled for joy. But by the afternoon they had all got anxious. Then a break in the clouds had revealed the two men in the couloir !

Victory

The night following that memorable assault was an unpleasant one for everybody on the South Col. In the overcrowded camp the men were sleeping up against the walls of the tents, and almost unprotected against the cold. A hurricane was blowing, and the temperature was − 13° (F.)

In the morning Hillary plucked up his courage, put on all his warm clothes, and slipped outside. Everest, blanketed in whirling, scurrying cloud, and with squalls whipping up flurries of snow on the ridges, was not an inviting sight. He staggered through the storm to Hunt's tent, where, after talking things over, the two men agreed to postpone the start twenty-four hours. This was regrettable, as one more day spent on the South Col could only result in accelerating physical deterioration among the party.

Towards noon Evans and Bourdillon left camp to go down for a rest, but shortly afterwards Evans returned alone to report that his companion was quite incapable of climbing the slope leading to the top of the Geneva Spur, even with the help of a fixed rope. It would be necessary to assist him if he were to be got to Base Camp. Hunt's intention had been to stay on the South Col throughout the second assault, for he remembered Longstaff's advice to him to take personal charge of the last camp. However, there could be no question of disorganizing the support party, so he put self last and went down, very much against his will.

All day the tempest howled over the South Col, attacking and destroying the morale of the men on it. Though Hillary and Tenzing entertained virtually no hope that the weather would improve, they nevertheless packed their kit for the morrow.

But the unexpected happened. On the morning of the 28th the wind slackened ; it did not drop, of course—it never drops on the South Col—but it became just sufficiently tractable for a start to be contemplated.

The plan was that Gregory, Lowe, and three Sherpas, with

Hillary and Tenzing following, should carry up on to the ridge the complement of stores needed for Camp 9. But unfortunately in the morning one of the Sherpas was found to be ill. His load had to be divided out among the others, which meant that Hillary and Tenzing would carry less oxygen. That was a really serious blow, for the rationing which such a shortage of gas would impose might well jeopardize the success of the expedition.

Round about nine o'clock the support party left camp, and an hour later the assault team moved off in its wake. At midday both groups met on the site of Lambert's camp, and halted. Though the remains of his little tent emphasized the desolation reigning in the place, the party were tempted to linger by the magnificence of the view. Eastward and westward it took in a vast horizon of snowy peaks which, seen from this height, still retained their grandeur as they reared their lofty shapes above plunging precipices.

A good 150 feet higher they found the dump Hunt had left ; each man took his share of these stores, and that brought their loads up to about 65 lb. each. Everything was not carried on the back ; odd articles were slung at their sides, while others protruded from their pockets, so that they looked like perambulating Christmas-trees.

The search then began for a tent-site. Not an easy job on the ridge, which rose steeply and uniformly without a break. Since there was no flat stretch, the support team came to the conclusion that one place was as good as another. But Hillary could always see the ideal spot a little higher up. . . . And when they came to it it was no more level than anywhere else.

It was a succession of disappointments ; the climbers were getting tired beneath their heavy burdens, and were wondering whether they would ever find what they were looking for, when Tenzing remembered having noticed a suitable patch somewhere about there. Leaving the ridge, he traversed to the left, and brought the procession to a rough platform under a rock-face. There the world's highest camp was pitched, at 28,200 feet. With evident pleasure the support party dropped their loads to the ground !

When the others had gone Hillary and Tenzing felt very much alone. But they had no time to let the feeling get the better of them, for they had plenty to do in putting their retreat in order. They first began to clear away the snow, laying bare a rocky ledge leaning towards a void. The south slope of Everest is decidedly no more favourable for camping than the north. Courageously taking up their axes, the two men prised out the stones cemented in by the frost. It was hard work, and they had to stop every

L

ten minutes to recover their breath. Two hours saw two strips levelled out, each measuring three feet by five and a half, one being a foot higher than the other. They somehow pitched their tent there, fastening the ropes to boulders or oxygen cylinders, because pegs could not be driven firmly into powdery snow.

Then Tenzing lit the stove and prepared the soup, while Hillary looked over the oxygen equipment. He was disturbed to find that the oxygen supply was smaller than he had thought, but nevertheless put aside a small reserve for the night.

Towards evening the wind slackened ; it became intermittent— that is, blowing in fierce gusts every ten minutes.

The two men put on all their warm clothes and turned into the tent, where they ate a substantial meal : sardines on biscuits, apricots in syrup—" heaven on earth," as Tenzing described them—dates, jam, honey, and plenty to drink.

Then Tenzing put down his inflated mattress on to the lower part of the platform, with part of it overhanging the void—a great void ! Yet the Sherpa lay down on it as calmly as if it had been a bed in an hotel room.

Hillary then tried to follow suit. He was on the higher portion of the platform, and as it was too small for him he had to remain half sitting, half lying ; the result was that a number of times during the night his leg fell on to his companion. Whenever he heard the wind blowing up he dug in his feet and shoulders to hold up the tent, as he had little confidence in its anchorages.

Despite the discomfort they slept, but only by breathing oxygen. At the rate of a litre a minute their stock would last four hours. Hillary had divided this into two periods, so that from nine to eleven, and from one to three, they were able to doze ; the rest of the night they were awake and suffering from the cold. The thermometer sank to $-17°$ (F.).

At four o'clock in the morning Hillary peeped out of the tent. The air was calm, and the sky wonderfully clear. Touched by the dawn, the great snowy peaks were the first to awake, above the still slumbering valleys plunged in shadow 17,000 feet below. Thyangboche monastery lay like a tiny pebble under grey water.

The two men began to make their final preparations. They lit the stove, ate their last box of sardines, and drank a great amount of lemonade to offset the loss of bodily moisture that lay ahead.

Hillary had trouble with his boots. They had been wet when he took them off the night before, and they were now frozen. He thawed them out over the Primus flame, regardless of the frightful smell of burning leather they gave off.

Six-thirty. They crawled out on all fours, roped up, charged their oxygen sets, and breathed a few draughts of the gas to pep themselves up a little. One for the road, so to speak.

Hillary did not feel entirely comfortable in his frozen boots, and so he asked Tenzing to take the lead for a start. So, kicking his way mightily through the deep snow, the Sherpa began to traverse upward towards the ridge on which the sun was glinting.

The first rays of the sun on a mountain are a kind of awakening, a deliverance, or like the opening of a flower. They are also a promise of the high adventure of sunny days on white peaks. . . .

Where the ridge narrowed to a knife-edge Hillary, whose feet were warm by now, took the lead, and the climb continued, slowly and surely.

When he arrived at the spot where Evans and Bourdillon had left their oxygen cylinders he stopped. He quickly scrutinized the gauge to see how much was left, and discovered with great joy that they still held a few hundred litres of gas, ensuring at any rate their ability to get back to the South Col. Relieved of a great source of anxiety, he moved on.

They were soon at the bottom of the long snowy slope leading to the South Summit. Like the earlier party, they found there thick powder-snow with a thin top-crust, and they too wondered if it would hold.

They might have taken the rocky route climbed by Evans and Bourdillon, but Hillary was primarily, like all New Zealanders, an ice mountaineer, and found it more natural to cut up the slope. Attacking it resolutely, he laboriously trod his way through the deep snow, not without feeling some qualms. At intervals Tenzing took over the lead. Once while Hillary was in front an area of the surface broke away round him, carrying him back a few yards— then miraculously stopping. This caused him to hesitate and consider the wisdom of going on after such a broad hint. The answer was pretty clear, but after all it was equally clear that Everest would not be climbed without taking risks. He consulted Tenzing, who admitted that the snow was very dangerous, but as he ended with his usual " Do as you like," [1] Hillary kept going.

The snow really was most unpredictable, because, after the warning that it might give way any minute, it held perfectly. And surprisingly enough, on the upper part of the slope it improved so much that they had to start cutting steps and fix on their crampons.

This eventually brought them to the South Summit by nine o'clock, and here they were confronted by that virgin ridge leading to the earth's highest summit. Did they see the blaze of glory

[1] Article entitled " The Conquest of Everest " in the newspaper *Figaro* of October 17–18, 1953.

surrounding it like a radiant sunrise, aflame with the cravings and burning thoughts of all who had endeavoured to conquer it ?

Not a bit of it ; their eager eyes were for other things, notably the ridge, which they scrutinized for weaknesses, weighing it up as one sizes up an opponent before a fight.

It wound up towards the blue sky beyond, with huge cornices projecting from it along the whole of its length. Yet its general appearance was less utterly unearthly than that of some Himalayan peaks, and it reminded one a little of an Alpine ridge. Still, Evans and Bourdillon were right ; it faced tired men with a formidable problem, and one which might well defeat them if the covering snow should not prove consistent. For it was unlikely that it would be possible to climb along the strip of sloping, stratified rock under-lying the cornices.

Farther up a wall of rock barred the way ; it was the step they had spotted through field-glasses at Thyangboche, and which even then had caused misgivings. Hillary realized that it could not be sized up from where they stood. That little bit that makes all the difference between the possible and the impossible can often only be seen at close quarters.

The two climbers hollowed out a seat just below the summit and took off their masks. That they could do so without suffocating is explained by the fact that they had so far kept their oxygen consumption low. Hillary looked over the sets, and worked out that if they continued to ration themselves they had enough left for four and a half hours' activity. Would that be enough to reach the summit and then come back down to the oxygen dump, he wondered. It is always hard to estimate how long it will take to climb a virgin ridge, and any attempt to do so may well be very wide of the mark when, as here, there is no certainty that the real top is visible.

But Hillary was climbing on, realizing that if there were any threat of oxygen shortage they must hurry. Besides, the sky was clear, and the weather quite exceptionally good. The mountain might all too soon begin to show its teeth again.

He was the first down from the South Summit. When he launched into the snow on the ridge he was overjoyed : it was hard and safe ! Two or three strokes with the axe were sufficient to cut a step. The snow was so well packed down, in fact, that the axe could be driven right in to the head to give a firm hold.

They advanced in turn, one feeding out rope from round his axe as the other moved up. They stayed as far as possible just below the crest of the ridge where the snow meets the rock. It is wise to maintain a margin of security when working on overhanging

A.J.N.

cornices, since one never knows just when or where they are likely to break off.

Conditions were excellent ; nevertheless, when Hillary, stepping lightly, removed his goggles to make a closer inspection he was immediately blinded by the driving snow. Although it could not be called a wind, there was a stiff breeze blowing, but they were both so well protected in their excellent climbing-suits that they did not feel either it or the cold.

Hillary suddenly noticed that Tenzing, who had up to then been going well, was beginning to slow down progressively. Suspecting that some fault in the Sherpa's oxygen equipment was at the bottom of this sudden show of fatigue, Hillary waited for him to come up. An inspection of the set revealed that he had not been mistaken : the oxygen pipe was almost completely blocked by ice. So, as a preventive measure, he cleaned out his own as well, in which the same thing was happening.

An hour's climb brought them to the base of the dreaded rock-step : a smooth wall nearly forty feet high cutting across the ridge. In Wales it would be a nice rock-climbing exercise ; at this altitude it was an impassable barrier. They therefore had to turn it. On the left nothing could be done, but on the right a snow cornice leaning against it was not quite flush with the rock. Between it and the wall of rock there was a narrow gap.

Hillary quickly made up his mind. With Tenzing belaying him he squeezed into the cleft, facing the rock, dug the heels of his crampons into the snow behind him, and started to climb. It was an awkward job, with a metal carrying-frame on his back and a mask over his face, but, using his knees, elbows, and shoulders, he pushed and hoisted himself upward, praying that the cornice would not give way under the pressure. He rose inch by inch, panting and leaden-limbed, and eventually got to the top, and with a final effort yanked himself on to the wall.

When he stood up he was all at once filled with a ferocious zeal, as if he had drawn fresh strength from the rock which had clasped him ; as if his tussle with the mountain had brought him a sudden revelation. He knew that victory lay within his grasp, he was sure that no obstacle could now hold him from the summit.

Then he planted himself firmly and brought Tenzing up, who likewise had a struggle and flopped down beside him, gasping like a great fish drawn from the depths.[1]

Then Hillary started cutting steps again. The ridge stood up

[1] It will be remembered that Tenzing's account of what happened in the final moments of the great victory differed somewhat from the above, which is based, of course, on Sir John Hunt's official report.—*Translator,*

British Base Camp on the Khumbu Glacier

with an air of finality against the sky, then curved over into another stretch, and finally reared up once more at the end of it, and so it went on. One hump seemed to beget a whole succession of others. Hoping to gain time, he tried just using crampons, but was quickly forced to give them up, as unsafe for tired climbers, and to continue cutting.

Tenzing was making slow progress, but every time Hillary asked him how he felt he smiled and motioned him on. So on they went, finding the task a dreary labour, largely because there were no specific difficulties to overcome. They felt weary, and fed up with that interminable ridge.

Hillary was wondering how much longer he would be able to hold out when suddenly in front of him the ridge began to descend. Down it swept, and at his feet he saw the North Col and the Rongbuk Glacier ! On the right a thin crest of snow rose towards a symmetrical white cone, perfectly formed, in every respect just what one would expect the highest point in the world to be. A few more strokes with their axes and they were there.

It was all over ! No more steps to cut, no more humps and obstacles to overcome ! The realization of that made them forget everything else, and brought a feeling of unspeakable relief.

Hillary looked at his watch ; it was half-past eleven. The ridge had taken two and a half hours to climb. He turned to Tenzing, and they shook hands. But under his mask the Sherpa's white teeth could be seen in a broad grin, and suddenly he threw his arms round Hillary and the two began to slap each other hard on the back until they had to stop for breath.

Hillary then took off his mask and looked round. The view was a little disappointing, because everything looked rather flat. All the mountains, great and small, were reduced to a common and uniform mediocrity. They had lost their individuality. They were now no more than crests in a white, heaving swell that went on for ever, cut up by glaciers.

Hillary's impression was similar to that experienced by people climbing Mont Blanc for the first time. They expect a stupendous view, and are disappointed at seeing in front of them only a wide, open sky, and at their feet a mass of anonymous peaks.

But on Everest the less remote landscape is still impressive. The North Face plunges into a bottomless abyss, and the East Ridge stretches endlessly, narrow, and indented with abrupt steps. Hillary thought of all those who had toiled up these routes, of Mallory and Irvine. He looked to see whether anything discarded on that ridge might betray the passing of the ill-fated pair. But there was nothing. Everest concealed her secret under a white-clad innocence, as at the beginning of things.

THE BRITISH EXPEDITION OF 1953

Delightedly Tenzing identified Rongbuk monastery in the north, deep in a brown valley, and pointed it out to his companion. Both to the north and to the south the two nearest inhabited places were two monasteries : Rongbuk and Thyangboche. Despite its forbidding harshness, the monks had sought out the closest possible proximity to this sublime spot. Perhaps they realized that thoughts were the more easily exalted where the gaze, too, could habitually be lifted to this acme of perfection, this point where intersect the soaring lines of a world the monks strive to transcend.

Being a devout Buddhist, Tenzing dug a hole in the snow and buried there his offering to the gods : chocolate, a packet of biscuits, and some sweets. And Hillary pushed down into the snow the little crucifix which Hunt had given him two days before, with the instruction to place it at the summit, if he got there.

Then he took some photographs. He had kept his camera warmly tucked inside his shirt throughout the ascent, and now he found difficulty in using it. Through being short of breath, he could hardly keep still while actually taking the picture. But he did take it, and it became famous as the one showing the Sherpa holding up aloft the flags of Great Britain, Nepal, India, and the United Nations. Then he walked round, but after ten minutes he noticed that his movements were gradually slowing down, so he replaced his mask, and immediately felt revived.

A quarter of an hour passed, and by then it was time to be thinking of the descent, as the oxygen cylinders had to be reached within a certain time. So they set off down. But ambition was no longer the spur, and their energy sagged, their legs felt weak, and their breathing was hurried. They fell into line again, and dropped from hump to hump, slithered down the ' chimney ' of rock and snow, traversed under the cornices, and in an hour were back at the South Summit.

There the fearsome snow-slope awaited them, and they became aware that this dangerous stretch had been on their minds throughout the ascent. As they entered on it their courage almost failed.

Hillary went down first. He did not throw all his weight on to alternate feet as is usual, but very carefully pressed the snow down with his foot to avoid setting it moving. What a long way 300 feet are when one is gripped by fear ! He took fresh heart by telling himself that every step was one more towards safety. Only 150 feet more . . . 100 . . . 50.

When they both reached the rocks again they looked into each other's eyes, and could each see the anguish the other had felt on that cruel stretch. It was fortunate that the terrain was becoming easier, for the nervous release made them feel all the more tired,

Tenzing on the Summit of Everest

which in turn made them all the more fallible. They picked up
the oxygen cylinders, and reached the tent. It was already drooping
and in a sorry state. The wind had tugged at it, and the ropes
were broken. There was just time to make some lemonade, change
the oxygen bottles, and rearrange their packs before dragging themselves off again, numb in body and mind, and walking as if in a
dream.

It needed a nasty surprise to bring them back to reality, and
the couloir provided it. The wind had blown hard and obliterated
all yesterday's steps. It was a case of cutting a fresh set, so they
began to hack away wearily, treading down each step, and then
using crampons. Meanwhile their stiff legs made them move like
wooden soldiers.

On the col the rest of the party were watching out for them.
As soon as Lowe and Noyce spotted them in the couloir they went
up to meet them with a fresh oxygen supply and hot soup. When
Hillary reached Lowe, who was hugging a Thermos of hot soup
to himself to keep it warm, he took off his mask and said, in a tone
of mingled surprise and incredulity, " Well, we've knocked the
bastard off ! " [1]

But the great joy of victory was for later, when the hardships
of that arduous day had been slowly forgotten.

[1] Quoted in a B.B.C. interview, July 24, 1953.

EPILOGUE

Borne on the ether, the news of victory reached London just in time for Queen Elizabeth's coronation, and all Britain was overjoyed.

But among mountaineers the feeling was rather one of surprise. It had become so customary for Everest expeditions to end in failure that it seemed that it must always be so. The future is all too readily pictured in terms of the past.

This expectation of failure was also attributable to the fact that the younger generation of British mountaineers were not well known. Those who had been climbing in the Alps since 1945, it was thought, were by no means out of the ordinary. They had performed no outstanding feats of mountaineering. It had so often been the case that the star climbers of the Welsh hills, when transferred to the Alps, had run into difficulties of route-finding, tricky snow, or loose rock to which they were unaccustomed, that there seemed little likelihood of finding among them men capable of solving a problem which had beaten so many famous pioneers.

Then, behold! every one was proved wrong, and it was revealed that Britain could boast mountaineers of the very first rank. At a stroke—and what a stroke!—they had restored British climbing to its place ahead of any other. It was amazing!

There were other reasons for astonishment, too. Had the Great Peak, which had so often turned attempts at conquest into tragedy, and even more often into dreadful ordeals, suddenly yielded of its own accord? And had the claims of justice moved it to grant victory to two men of the two nations which, by effort and sacrifice, had most richly deserved this reward : the British and the Sherpas ? It was almost too good to be true. But the good sometimes *is* the true.

Everest took care to give its story a fitting ending, and we should be grateful for that. What does the future hold in store for this mountain ? Will it see many more mountaineers ? Or will it remain in splendid isolation in cold, in rarefied atmosphere, and in wind ? None can say. It seems certain, at all events, that its height will preserve it from the common fate which decrees, according to Mummery, that every mountain which is regarded as unclimbable later becomes " an easy day for a lady." Whatever its future, it will have provided some of us with the opportunity of performing one of those fine feats which are, after all, not so vain, since they show what enthusiasm and stubborn courage can do, when intelligence directs them.

The Great Peak has earned men's gratitude in bringing its epic to a close under a cloudless sky, on a matchless day, and with the goodwill of us all. It might be said that two men only reached the summit. But this is not so, for morally all those whose hopes, these many years, bore them on towards the topmost cone of white have trodden it with phantom feet. All were there, the men of to-day and of yesterday, the living and the dead.